THE BUSINESS MINDED CREATIVE

How to live a fulfilling creative life and make money

DIANA WINK

The Business Minded Creative

Book One in the Books for Storytellers Series

Cover Design by David Rodrigues

To all my mentors who have inspired and taught me
because a small action can have an enormous impact.

Contents

Part IV
The three pillars of a future-proof creative

PART I

The Call to Adventure

Are your tired?

My shoe sole clung to the sticky floor of the tram as the automatic doors' attempt to close failed yet again. This was the worst night of my life. Fourteen hours ago, I had stumbled through my front door, sleepy and hazy, to get to my day job. The commute took two hours, usually.

Now I was on my way back, stuck in that tram. Undecided whether to scream at the drunk people blocking the tram door on every single station to Cologne central, or to just burst out crying, I just stood there, taking in the disgusting smell. It was the night of carnival. Surrounded by a dressed up and hammered crowd, I just wanted to get home.

The train I normally boarded, the one that took me straight to my hometown, had stopped on a station somewhere in Cologne. After an hour, the conductor announced we wouldn't be moving, advising to take the tram to the main station. Another hour later, I arrived at Cologne central, only to wait for an additional thirty minutes and board *the exact same* train I had left behind on that station in the middle of nowhere.

When I arrived in Dusseldorf, I walked over to the platform to wait for yet another train, collapsed in a metal cold seat and allowed tears to freely stream down my cheeks. I was tired. Cold. Frustrated.

Today, I am thankful for that night. It had brought something to the surface that had been sitting inside for a long time. In the past six months, I have lived a mere existence. I didn't hate my job. In fact, it was a very prestigious position in an advertising agency. I had the privilege to nearly run the whole video department. But I hated the chains it had put on me.

I got up early, commuted, sat in the office or did shootings, sometimes even did nothing, just to kill time and justify the working hours, then another two hours to return home, grab some dinner and go to bed. I was caught up in a wheel that wouldn't stop turning. And I was lucky enough to disembark early, thanks to this fateful, devastating night that threw me over the edge.

I quit my day job the next day.

Maybe you're not that lucky. Maybe you've pondered about quitting for years. But your commute only takes thirty minutes, the office is pleasant and has free coffee, and the pay is good. You've had a raise or two. Are hoping for a higher position. If you quit now—was all of this for nothing? All these years, wasted?

Most who get to pursue their artistic dreams are thrown into it with a lucky punch. Madonna lost her job at Dunkin Donuts, Robert Redford was found asleep at Standard Oil and smashed several glasses before he was let go, and J. K. Rowling was fired from her job as a secretary. Sometimes, the minor comforts and the enormous timespan we've been in the jobs forced upon us become our chains. Just another year until I can save up a little. The kids will go to college soon. The boss promised me a raise if I keep up the excellent work.

Or maybe you find yourself at the other end of the spectrum. The one I found myself in three years later, when I called my husband and uttered the words: *I'm tired of living this way.*

It was a frosty autumn morning.

Drizzling rain, dark grey clouds and a chilly wind that made an unsettling sound around our windows. My husband was on a short lunch break while we talked on the phone. My one-year-old daughter was running circles around me. I stared at our bank balance. A huge debt stared back at me, like a familiar house guest bidding its greetings.

As usual, I was in a hurry—drop off my toddler at daycare to start writing novel #4. But writing was not on my radar. It felt forced. Have I ever loved it? When scraping money for groceries, creating seems redundant. *I'm tired of living this way*. This was what I said to him. My husband didn't reply. But he, too, knew that something had to change. That I was on the edge of giving up.

As you've probably already guessed, I quit my day job to start a life as a vigilante. Fresh meat on the savannah of freelancers. I set out to write novels while working as a freelance filmmaker. Married. Had a beautiful baby daughter. And was tired as hell from doing and being… everything. A filmmaker, writer, podcaster, YouTuber (as a film school graduate, it was my duty to be on YouTube), blogger, mom, homemaker, wife, and honorary local musical director.

On top of all of that, there was always too much month left at the end of the salary. I was tired of my parents urging me to get a "proper job" because after all, I had a Master's degree. I was tired of not being able to afford vacations and time-off because as I freelancer, none of those get paid.

I'm tired of living this way.

Whatever the situation you find yourself in professionally, if this is what the small voice inside of you whispers in your quiet moments or when the stress of everyday life abounds—I've been there. I know exactly what you're feeling. A sense of fear. A shadow of hopelessness. Burnout. Depression. Or just this notion that something is off. That you've buried your dreams somewhere deep and reality just won't allow them to the surface.

Something needs to change. But how?

This is what this book is about. Consider it an (entertaining and highly practical) instruction manual to live the life of your creative dreams. It is possible. Just not in the way you think.

And I hope this change will begin with this book. Like mine began with a fateful conversation that altered my creative path forever. A conversation with Joanna Penn.

The gift of perspective

It was a hot day. One of those where sweat drips down your forehead from just sitting around. I was hammering my fingers against the desk, staring at the Zoom conference about to begin.

This madness started with an email.

When I wrote that email several weeks before, I was ready for rejection. Joanna Penn, the person behind The Creative Penn, has been my online mentor for years. I've been listening to and supporting her podcast, buying most of her books in print to put them on my shelf; but her last course was the one that affected me the most.

I wrote an email, asking her to come on my podcast. Joanna always answers emails, so it was a relief that I wouldn't have to wait for weeks, wondering if an answer would even come. Still, I expected she would decline politely. My podcast audience was small to non-existent. I still made my case in a carefully worded text and pressed SEND. On the next day, the answer came.

Why was I so afraid to open it? I guess rejection scares all of us. That's why we don't even try. Her answer was a simple: *Of course, I'd love to be on your show :)*

I could have done somersaults across the room. At the same time, it dawned on me: *You'd have to talk to Joanna Penn.* Joanna. Penn. I definitely had to prepare for the interview, mentally, I mean. The topic of the episode: **How to balance business and creativity.**

What I did not know was that this conversation would change my creative endeavors forever. And this change began with a challenge.

What do you think about money?

We decided to publish the interview in audio only, guessing nobody wanted to see our faces glistening with sweat. Joanna challenged the audience with questions around creativity and business, yet all this time, it felt like she was challenging me.

> "What do you believe in? What projects do you love? What won't let you go? And at the same time, how can you serve your audience, your readers, your fans? And combining both of them and also taking risks is something that we creatives do."
>
> "We all think that there's a magic bullet, but actually I think the struggle is just the journey. And if you're not struggling financially, then you'll be struggling with your story. Because if you're not struggling with your story, then you're not challenging yourself enough. And you know what, at the end of the day, it has to be, or else everyone would do it."
>
> "It can be very hard to face up to some of the things that you think about money, you feel about money, and that will really hold you back big time. That would be my challenge for you and people listening. If you can't say out loud, I want to be a wealthy author, I want to be a six-figure author, I want to be a seven-figure author, I love money – that's really hard for people to say. I practice, you see. Then you will struggle to bring it in."
>
> *—Joanna Penn on the Story Artist Show.*

Joanna's greatest gift to me was perspective. Another—more mature—perspective on my creativity. A challenge to combine my creativity and business into a focused ecosystem.

Most creative people are the same: we have so many awesome things we want to do that we tend to scatter all over the place. It's hard to find focus. On top of that, we are told that we need to be everywhere. On every new and upcoming platform. Provide content everywhere at the same time. Regularly. In high quality. We need to compete for the limited attention customers are ready to give. Where to start? What to do? What will work, and what won't? You can only find out by trying, right? And until then, you're slowly burning out.

Joanna asked me a very important question: **What do you think about money?** It startled me. Money was… just money. Great if it's there. But I'm not crazy about it. It's not my goal to have a lot of money. After all, I wouldn't have become a creative freelancer. Nobody does *this* for money.

And this is what creatives mostly are like. We just want enough to get by. Not to starve would be great. We need little as long as we can do what we love. The problem is: this is how we approach our creativity. We don't really care about money, although it would be awesome to make a little. How? We don't have a clue. If some people bought our book—great. We even go as far as feeling guilty to charge for what we have produced. We price the things free or as low as possible because we feel like impostors. Who am I to charge this amount of money for my work? I'm not Michelangelo. Nor Stephen King.

We feel like a charity case, grateful if people even consider donating something for our efforts. Because in the back of our heads, our creations are not worth paying for, they cannot compete with the stuff that the masters have birthed.

This mindset is devastating. Most creatives undervalue their work, thus bringing down the market and putting themselves on a path to burnout. If we don't learn to like money—here, I said it—we won't ever have a sustainable creative career.

After the interview, I felt as if at a crossroad for several weeks. Pondering. Regularly scribbling ideas, musings, and finally a business plan. I suddenly felt like I was given a navigation map. A path to follow with a distinct road ahead. What this conversation started and the following weeks and months continued was a profound mind shift and a practical roadmap.

With creativity and business, we need a mind shift. Without it, our efforts will be pointless. If you're not ready to at least consider this, you might as well flush your work down the drain and go back to your day job. For your own sanity's sake. Before you end up like Van Gogh—alcohol abuse, rejection, neglected mental and physical health. To become a thriving, happy artist—and yes, this is possible—you need to deeply challenge your misconceptions about creativity and money. And this will be our first step in this book.

This is never easy, and it's a process that takes commitment and patience. But if you expect lasting change, if you expect your understanding to deepen, you need to become an archeologist—ready to dig deeper. Challenge your thinking. Reveal secrets long hidden and put them into context.

Have you ever watched the movie "Tenet" by director Christopher Nolan? The first time you watch it, your head is spinning, and the brain feels like mush. But if you don't give up right there, and doom the movie as being too complicated, you get the satisfaction of watching it again and experiencing one aha-moment after the other. Like in a math exercise, where you read, and re-read, and try to solve the problem until days or weeks later, the solution comes to you. This aha-moment is always worth fighting for, because is deepens your understating and opens up new perspectives. But it never comes easy. It requires blood, sweat and time.

Change won't come easy. But it will come if you dig deeper. As you face your fears, doubts and lies you believed subconsciously, you gradually become another person. As you change your daily practices according to your beliefs, you will become a better creative. A person able to reach your personal definition success.

This book focuses on deepening your understanding and shifting your mindset about artistic business on the one hand while building on this foundation in your day-to-day life. Ready to dig deeper?

Change your day

> "Success is the product of daily habits—not once-in-a-lifetime transformations."
>
> James Clear, *Atomic Habits*

A newspaper in Michigan published the following story: On a business trip in terrible weather, Mr. Blue had the impression that his windscreen wipers couldn't cope with the rain. He stopped, opened the car door—and had to swim for fifty meters to get out of the lake he had driven into.

This true anecdote reveals a very important principle. When you focus on your goal, the place you want to get to at all costs, you end up getting out of the car far too late. You are blind to the problems until you're drowning in them. Why? Because you don't stop regularly to question your methods. Your systems. Stopping now might be too high a cost. You want to get to your goals fast. The instant noodle and Amazon Prime world urges you every single day to just keep moving.

I've been there before my conversation with Joanna. Drowning in tasks, trying to catch up with those who have been in the business for over ten years. Write the next book. Produce the next course. Learn marketing. Email regularly. Do Facebook ads. Publish a podcast episode every week.

Why do we get tired? Why do we lose the fascination over the one thing that we once loved so dearly? We get busy. And while yes, you should consider your creative endeavor a job and turn up every day, the question is: how effective is what you're doing?

If a plane flies from point A to point B and only changes its trajectory very slightly, it will wind up thousands of kilometers away from where it was headed to. Ask yourself: the little things that you're doing day in, day out, when you turn up, when you do your creative work—where are they *really* taking you?

Adjust your trajectory by adjusting your daily habits. We live life day by day, season by season and year by year. But what you do with every single day will accumulate towards your destination. Life is not lived in single grand moments despite Hollywood movies portraying it this way. Yet subconsciously, this shapes our culture and our expectation to life. Daily activities are boring. What we instead desire is this magical, transformational moment.

This is a lie. Life doesn't work that way, and if you keep waiting for this moment, you'll look back at your wasted years with regret. What you need to learn instead, if you want to savor your days to their fullest, is how to live the everyday life in an effective, creative, and sustainable way—when to create, when to do business, how to plan your day in order to see success, how to plan your month and quarter and year in order to get where you want to go.

When you have established the foundation of the mind change concerning creativity and business, you need to plan your days in the most effective way and establish the necessary habits. This book will get you there. At least on paper. You must execute the work. We will look at scientific research, consider other sources and the lives of famous creatives. I will share my own experiences and how I've altered and still am altering my everyday life to reach my goals without burning out. Creativity is about play. Business is about calculation. And you need to sail right through the middle for a thriving creative life.

In the following part of the book, we'll start with creativity—how to find your creative sweet spot, how to stay playful in your everyday life, and how to establish a daily practice for creativity. The third part of the book deals with business, how to transform it into your perfect creativity radar, how to incorporate business into your every day life and write your creative business plan. Finally, the last part is an outlook into the future of creativity and what you can do to prepare.

I hope you're as excited as I am to dive in. Because like the conversation with Joanna Penn, this book might change your creative life.

The waters are waiting.

PART II

Creativity

The Sweet Spot

"You are never too old to set another goal or to dream a new dream."

C. S. Lewis

My daughter has just turned two. Last night, she took the finger painting cans, put them on top of each other to build a "house", on top of them the wooden letters of the alphabet—which together looked like a huge, multicolored tower. She grabbed her two teddy bears, one in each hand, put on some music, and started running around the "house", singing.

Nobody taught her to do this. She came up with this all by herself, repurposed the cans without wondering if this was "supposed to be that way". She was not ashamed to dance and sing, celebrating her creation. Her expression was pure delight, especially when she saw me and could present her accomplishment with pride.

I'm not telling you this to propose my daughter is a creative genius. On the contrary. She's a typical two-year-old. Which shows that creativity sits within every single one of us. And it brings an enormous amount of delight—in the process, and when shared with others. We were made for creativity. And we can see it plainly in children.

But society devours this creativity if our parents don't take an effort to let it flourish within us. And as a parent, I now know that it takes a tremendous amount of effort. Children's creativity is under attack. They are not supposed to do this and have to do that. There is always "the right way" to do things. And you want them to learn the right way, don't you? Besides, creative endeavors at home mean a colossal mess. Which is inconvenient. Which demands your time and attention. Time that we are expected to invest into teaching them reading and math, not watching them stack paint cans.

If I'm not purposeful about my daughter's creativity, life will crush it. So chances are that your parents probably just didn't have the means to preserve and encourage your creativity. Or somewhere along the lines, people told you you weren't creative. And you believed it.

There's the other end of the spectrum. You recognize that you're creative, but like most artists, you are interested in *everything.* You tried several things, but you just can't focus. Or you're constantly asking yourself—am I really in my creative sweet spot? Like Jack Sparrow's compass, your creativity might run in circles without a clear direction. You need to readjust your trajectory. Maybe a lot. Maybe just a little.

Welcome to the Creative Sweet Spot Diagramm—a very simple yet effective exercise to find your creative sweet spot. For this, just grab a notebook or a big piece of blank paper, a pen or pencil, and perhaps some quality coffee (seriously, pour the instant coffee down the drain) —and let's get started.

Your Creative Sweet Spot Diagramm

With creative endeavors, most people are just told: *Do what you love.* This is as unhelpful as letting a toddler pick her own outfit from the entire wardrobe. She'll be going through the clothes and trying them on for hours. Or she'll just want to wear a winter jacket on a hot summer day.

If you're serious about your creativity (which is a contradiction, because what's serious about creativity?), passion is not enough. You need two other ingredients, and your Sweet Spot is a place where those three ingredients overlap perfectly:

1. Your experience
2. The world's needs
3. Your passion

1. Your experience

This quest begins with an adventure into your past. And my past was possibly the most enlightening adventure that brought me into my current creative endeavor. But first, let's look at the lives of three very interesting people.

Alexander Niehues (aka Alex Newton) worked as a senior management consultant in the corporate world for 20 years. Twenty. Years. He has worked his way up. Got the prestigious job. It would be insanity to quit, right?

But sometimes, it's the only sane thing to do. Alex quit his career to work at home in Stuttgart and founded K-lytics—a revolutionary platform with in-depth reports on various genres and sub-genres on Amazon. Maybe it has been his dream all along. But what's more likely is the fact that these years in consulting gave him the knowledge and ability to go out on his own and start this amazing company.

Brad Andalman and Brad West worked for a combined thirty years at Pixar Animation Studios where they helped create Pixar's feature films and develop its next generation animation software. This sounds like an awesome job.

> "Brad and I worked on the next generation animation system at Pixar, and we put a lot hours into that and feel like we both contributed a huge amount to that piece of software, but that's still Pixar's thing and this is our thing."
>
> Brad Andalman on The Creative Penn Podcast

While the yearning for something that was their own and also a good amount of savings gave them the courage to leave, their experiences that Brad "wouldn't trade for anything"—the fact that they created software for creative people—contributed a big deal to the product that every self-published author now talks about and has on their Mac: Vellum.

I didn't spend decades in the corporate world. But I still graduated in a different field. When I finished my Master's Degree in Film Directing, I wanted to be like Christopher Nolan. Filmmaking was and still is one of my greatest passions. But things didn't come together the way I imagined them to. I grew frustrated and wondered what the heck to do with my life until I have the magical breakthrough as a Hollywood film director (hint: it probably will never come, at least not from waiting).

My past forced me to examine what exactly I loved about filmmaking. Looking back, I saw how I was writing short stories and poems as early as seven years old (which I now thought were pretty good for a child that age). I wrote my first novel when I was eleven. And even in film school, I wrote scripts equal to the screenwriting students. I saw a pattern emerge. My love for storytelling. And I realized that at that time, writing was my best option—the one that would allow me to live my ideal daily life (working remotely) and gave me the most control over my success (in film, you need a budget for everything). What started out as my graduation short movie became an amazing trilogy of full-length novels read by thousands.

Examine your past. The good and the ugly. See if you can spot a pattern. What have you enjoyed doing? What have you naturally been good at? Nothing in your past is wasted – your engineering degree, your decade-long career in a day job, your years of being a stay-at-home mom.

Brad Pitt for example worked at El Pollo Loco chicken restaurant where he had to dress as a chicken and try to get a passerby to eat in the restaurant—probably this was when he discovered his love for acting? Your experiences shape you into the person you are today. They provide you with an endless well you can pull from, and at the same time, they can illuminate the way into the future.

The knowledge you gained will set you apart from others. I have started a writing career, but my unique knowledge in technology and film helps me create book trailers and unique YouTube videos. Where other authors struggle with beautiful imagery and professional looking videos as they dabble into YouTube, I have the advantage that I can create unique moving picture experiences for my audience. And I never underestimate this advantage.

Too often, we focus on the things we don't know. You can certainly learn what you don't know—but it takes time. Instead, focus on what you've learned in all those years and the advantages it can provide you with. Nothing you've learned, no skill you gained, should be wasted. What is your unique set of experiences and knowledge?

2. The World's Need

> "If you want to love what you do, abandon the passion mindset ("what can the world offer me?") and instead adopt the craftsman mindset ("what can I offer the world?")."
>
> Cal Newport, So Good They Can't Ignore You

Creativity is a service. And while we will go deeper into that aspect in the business section of the book, it is important to gain the right perspective on your trajectory.

My heart lights up when I get emails from my readers. Even small things like the fact that I've made their day or inspired them with my content—my email newsletter, my podcast episode, or my online course.

Our creativity comes alive in the hands of our audience. If you constantly shout into the wind, and only an empty echo returns, you will burn out. Nothing drains the creative passion like not making any kind of difference. And while many consider art inherently self-centered—just imagine this typical artist in his cave, painting or carving throughout the night like a madman until a masterpiece emerges, something that looks therapeutic and ecstatic—the truth is that the awe of an audience fuels creativity. When it changes the mind and heart of another, and like an avalanche, starts a movement.

So when considering your creative trajectory, you always should take the world's need into consideration, and your view of it. Because all of us look at the world differently. And see things that are missing, or could be improved. Think:

- *What is lacking in this world?*
- *What is most needed?*
- *Where do you see a vacuum that needs to be filled?*

3. Your passion

If you're like many creative people, it's hard to pick one single passion at the beginning. For the sake of this exercise, you are allowed pick several. Write down everything you are passionate about. Everything that makes your heart light up on fire. The things that don't let you sleep at night, that you ponder over in your daydreams. What is the special group of people you care about? Children, young adults, creative people, parents or singles, teachers, scientists? What are the special areas of life and/or work that you just can't stop thinking about? Books, travel, sports, medicine, technology, or board games? Write it all down.

Reflect whether this interest is something you could pursue for the next ten or twenty years. When I gave birth to my daughter, I was so passionate about babies—baby sleep, baby food, working out with babies, toddler parenting. And I'll be honest, the thought of starting a mommy blog crossed my mind. But I had to put it aside because it was not an evergreen interest. It would pass as soon as my child left this stage—which happens faster than you realize Be honest with yourself about the things that might just be a phase, and those you've been passionate about you for years.

At this stage, allow yourself to be abstract in order to generate more ideas instead of constraining yourself. Don't think about a product yet. Think about a lifestyle. A creative adventure that you're ready to embark on for the long term. A direction.

What are your deepest passions?

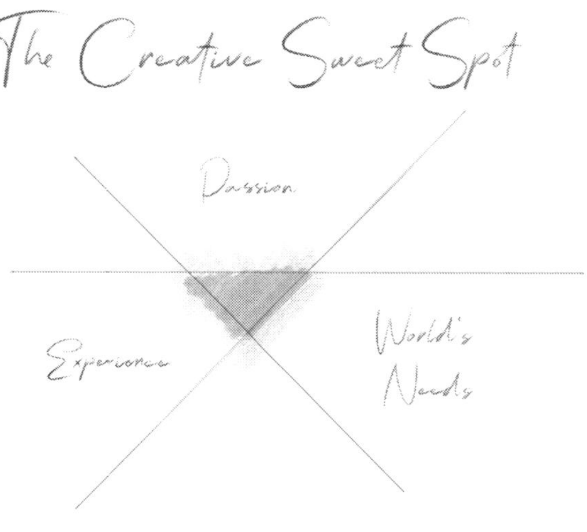

Your Sweet Spot—the Intersection

Your Creative Sweet Spot is where those three things intersect: your experience, the world's needs, and your passion. The place where all of those meet is the perfect direction for your creative endeavor. A combination of those three will give you a proper compass to direct you on this adventure. You'll need it more often than you know; in the beginning stage when your creative business is formed, and every time you will need to readjust your trajectory. Which for me happens at least once every year. Maybe even several times throughout the year.

You always must pivot your creative projects, measure your ideas against your creative direction in order to decide whether you're walking the right paths. You must turn around. Maybe throw away finished products and re-start. This is why this exercise is so important. It will be a guide and remind you why you're doing this, and where you need to go if you've fallen off track.

Find the intersection. Discover your sweet spot.

And let's embark on the adventure of your lifetime.

Learning Islands

The World Economic Forum Human Capital Outlook Report predicts that "disruptive changes to business models will have a profound impact on the employment landscape over the coming years." The same report estimates that "65% of children entering primary school today will ultimately end up working in completely new jobs that don't yet exist."

While it makes me anxious and excited for my kids, it also tells me that the world is constantly changing. New trends and technologies emerge every second. Machine Learning, Cloud Computing, The Internet of Things, Voice Technologies and Augmented Realities—those things develop faster than we can keep up with.

Therefore, in order to become a successful artist, you need to never stop evolving—both in your craft and in current developments in your field. But with all the work that you need to do, where to even find the time to learn? Before we jump into the section that teaches you how to establish a daily creative practice, I want to introduce a concept that has helped me accumulate knowledge and become a constant well of ideas.

I call it the "Learning Islands".

How much time do you waste daily?

And I don't even mean your Netflix binge in the evenings or the Instagram scrolling when you've finally hit the couch. This is not the topic of this book (which is a shame, because I have a lot to tell about that). I mean the time you don't know you have.

Michael Laronn, author of 45 books, YouTuber, podcaster, speaker... you name it, says: "30% to 40% of my writing is done on my phone." Because he works a lot of hours on his day job, has a young family, a puppy and a rabbit, and on top of all of that is in law school (I know, how the heck has he written 45 books?), Michael needed a way to keep his daily word count up. So he wrote novels on his phone; while in the backseat of an Uber, waiting in the doctor's office, standing in line at the grocery store.

> "And all those little writing sessions, it might be two or three minutes at a time, they add up in a really, really big way over the day. [...] I've reclaimed time during the day that I would not normally have been able to write."
>
> Michael Laronn on The Creative Penn Podcast

The minutes add up. And while Michael writes during those minutes, I'm an advocate to do creative work in another way, a way that allows you to do what Cal Newport calls "Deep Work", and we will talk about this in the next chapters. Laronn's habit illustrates another point. It shows that throughout the day, we have wasted time windows that accumulate to hours. Hours that can be used for a better purpose. And I prefer to use them for learning.

Those are my daily **Learning Islands**. They happen while I drive to work, when I have my lunch break and go out for coffee, while I do dishes or prepare breakfast. As you might have already guessed, I mostly learn and stay up to date through audio: podcasts and audio books. They are the easiest way to consume. But I also have a paperback book on my nightstand which I read and mark up every night before bed (this is my way of trying to escape the Netflix black hole). A couple of years ago, I was not a podcast fan. But after some getting used to, I realized how convenient audio content is, and was converted.

Where are your Learning Islands? What are the things you do daily that you could use to consume books and podcasts and elevate your knowledge in your creative field? Commute is probably the best one. Household chores and things that need to be done but don't require thinking are also a good way to go. Every line, doctor's waiting room or traffic jam.

Download some books to your phone, pick some podcasts or, if it's an activity where you can and prefer to read like riding a train, download some ebooks. And every time you see a Learning Island coming —use it.

Don't forget to daydream

Unfortunately, I took this principle to an extreme one year, so here's a word of caution:

Daydreaming and boredom are very important ingredients to a creative life. Those are the things we have forgotten in an always-on-world. And while it's better to listen to a book rather than scroll the Instagram feed, sometimes it's best to just put the phone away entirely. Embrace the boredom. Stop constantly filling yourself with *stuff.*

Let your thoughts dance in the air while you watch the particles being caressed by the early sunlight and inhale the smell of freshly brewed coffee (remember, the good stuff, not the instant garbage). Watch your kids' concentrated play as you observe their every feature, grin and eye-roll, and count yourself the luckiest person in the world. Inhale your surroundings, listen, feel and just be. This is the stuff from which ideas are made. These are the moments that allow our subconscious to process and resurface with something that feels like the kiss of the muse.

Why did the poets of old walk for hours on end? Charles Dickens took 1,5-hour long vigorous walks every day, Tchaikovsky took a 1-hour walk, as did Beethoven and Victor Hugo. John Milton walked for two hours up and down his garden, from 6.30 to 8.40 p.m. What did he do with this time? There were no headphones, no music or podcasts he could listen to while he walked. He did nothing. And this was the secret. As Nietzsche said: "It is only ideas gained from walking that have any worth."

To be productive, we try to fill every second of our time with content and knowledge, but those voices drain us instead. Get away from the consumption regularly, schedule leisurely walks in the park, savor the time with your kids instead of picking up the phone and checking work-related messages, allow your thoughts to wander and allow boredom to enter the stage. It will not only make you a happier and better person, but it will make you a better artist because "to think original thoughts, we must put a stop to constant stimulation" (Manoush Zomorodi, Bored and Brilliant).

> "When our minds wander, we activate something called the "default mode," the mental place where we solve problems and generate our best ideas, and engage in what's known as "autobiographical planning," which is how we make sense of our world and our lives and set future goals."
>
> Manoush Zomorodi, Bored and Brilliant

How often do you let your mind wander? How often do you allow yourself to do nothing and just be in the moment? This is a crucial skill we have forgotten, but since I started practicing it purposefully, I sensed that time stopped "flying". It slowed down, just for me, and it helped get so much more clarity in my everyday life and my creativity, which is neatly tied to the health of our souls.

Fall in love with the Learning Islands. Pick meticulously what you want to consume during those precious minutes. But also, give yourself time to be utterly off grid and just inhale life. And for the sake of all that is holy, delete social media and every other devourer of your precious time.

The Daily Creative Practice

Mozart wrote to a friend: "People err who think my art comes easily to me. I assure you, dear friend, nobody has devoted so much time and thought to composition as I."

For my podcast, I had the privilege to interview self-publishing sensation Hugh Howey, a leader to the new paradigm of publishing, and a success story with his *Wool* book series. The film rights are already sold to 20th Century Fox. Hugh lives on a boat and sails the world as he continues to write. But his outlook on creativity is extraordinary. His general rule is: **work harder than anyone else.**

> "And where it really adds up, it's not just having a three-hour session one day. It's when you can do three hours every day habitually. And for me, that meant getting up an hour early.
>
> I would go to work and sit in a bookstore that wasn't open yet, completely dark. Just sit there with my laptop and have an hour and a half or two hours before the first people showed up. And then an hour on my lunch break and then try to go home and get 30 minutes to an hour in before I went to bed.
>
> If you do that every single day, the hours really add up. If

> you just do it one day and then take four days off, you'll never get those days back. And I think consistency is the key to producing not only a lot of work, but your best work."
>
> Hugh Howey on the Story Artist Podcast

Your life's situation is unique. But we all have a lot on our plate. Nobody has time to spare. We're busier than people ever were. I've never met anybody who said: "I've so much time, I don't know what to do with it.". The key to producing your best creative work in a sustainable way lies in using your daily time wisely. Nobody has more time than the other, it's the one thing we all have in common. 24 hours. For all of us. The key to using those hours to your advantage is purposefulness. **A daily practice.**

It doesn't have to be the 3-4 hours Hugh Howey put in before he could live from his writing. If you have kids, this is not even possible. But even if you start with a daily fifteen minutes, and build this habit, you'll see what an enormous difference it makes. Let's throw away the misconceptions about this one fateful night where the neurotic but ecstatic artist (probably on drugs, or at least drunk) paints a masterpiece or writes the best novel of all times. This is neither a healthy way to live, nor a realistic depiction of the creative process. If you spend your days waiting for this moment, you'll fail.

The creativity is inside of you already. But ideas are worth nothing. Everybody has ideas. The execution makes the difference. The faithfulness to show up daily and do the work is what will get you into the flow state and help you produce extraordinary creative work. There are scientific hacks to help you get into this flow state, which we will talk about in the next chapters. But here, I want you to just realize that in order to become a successful and fulfilled artist, you must enter the uncomfortable (at least in the beginning) zone of habit.

It won't crush your creativity. Creativity is not about chaos and being disorganized. People who excuse their messiness with being "an artist" have it all wrong. The framework of a habit will make your creativity flourish and the consistency of a daily practice will get you into the state of flow, a state where the best work is produced. Contrary to society's assumptions, we find creativity in boredom, repetition, time-pressure and consistency.

Does this blow your mind? Does it discourage you? If you're like me, dreaming about this unpredictable, ecstatic life of an artist, this harsh reality might put you off. But don't give up this dream just yet. The unpredictable discovery, the play and sudden epiphany are still part of the process. You'll still laugh, cry, and marvel with the ideas you'll come up with. The difference lies in the fact that these ideas are earned. A lot of work goes into solving the problem and coming up with hundreds of bad ideas before you finally get a good one. The difference is that you'll know how to handle these ideas and put them into practice, get them out into the world to find an audience and a life of their own.

Mozart knew a secret nobody likes to promote: devotion to the daily practice is inevitable to become a remarkable artist. But how can you build this daily practice? What should it look like? And how can you integrate it into your already busy day? We will talk about all of this in the next chapters.

The Creative Habit

What's a habit? And why is it so important to establish one?

A habit is an action that is repeated enough times to become automatic.

And automatic is the key word here. Why would an artist want to automate anything?, you'd ask. Rightly so, because we like to assume that masterpieces are born from spontaneity and chaos. But please, remember Mozart.

A creative habit is different. It sets the framework and provides the security for the creative mind to flourish and work. But more than that, a habit forms the person you want to become.

We structure our lives in days. Every morning, we get a new chance. But we don't start from the day scratch. Our life is the sum of the actions and decisions from the preceding years. So while the new day is a chance to do well or screw up, it's still painting on the canvas of the years that have gone before. If you screw up for one day, it doesn't matter in light of the bigger picture. But if you screw up day after day, the effects will accumulate. Similarly, you won't get fat by eating one burger just like you won't get thin by eating one salad. The results always lie in the sum.

This is where the habit comes into play. Small daily habits build into compounds that make up our life. Those habits define who we are and what the course of our lives will become. Remember the analogy of the plane trajectory? This is the same with our lives. Deviate for a short time and then get back on track—nothing happened. Deviate from the trajectory for a longer period, and you will land somewhere else entirely. The longer you deviated, the longer it takes to get back to your destination. In conclusion, a real habit is not about what you want to do, but about the person you want to become.

We form habits throughout life. We can't help it. It's just the way our brain is wired. The problem is: most habits that we form unconsciously are unhelpful, even destructive habits. Biting the nails. Procrastinating. Scrolling social media. Our brain is enchanted by the lure of the moment, disregarding where the habit will get us in the long run. In order to take back control of our lives, we need to take control of our habits and instill positive habits into the daily routine that will get us where we want to go. Trick our brains, so to speak.

The creative habit is the most important one of all. It's the time where you **create**, purposefully setting yourself apart from others who have fallen victim to consumerism. This is the time where you strive to produce meaningful work. Where you get away from consumption and reactive behaviour, and commit to creating meaningful work that might change the world.

The beauty: once it's automatic, you get the decision-making process out of the way and focus on the actual creative work. We all wrestle with the inner procrastinator or the small voice that whispers: *just stay in bed for a few more minutes.* An established habit takes this out of the equation. It gets you to the results faster and helps you get into the creative flow with less traction.

Creating this habit itself is far from painless. It will come at a cost, and it will demand your time and energy at the beginning. But fear not. We will use scientific hacks to create the perfect habit that is easy, attractive and satisfying, thus signaling to your brain to get more of it. And when you look back at your life months and years from now, years where you refused to give up, stayed on track more days than strayed, you will marvel at what even fifteen minutes a day can do.

It's all in the emotions.

Did you know that your habit to brush the teeth was orchestrated by the prominent advertising executive, Claude C. Hopkins?

About a hundred years ago, no one brushed their teeth. But when Hopkins heard about a new toothpaste called Pepsodent, he thought he could make a killing. Before scientists have ever proven how a habit is formed, Hopkins knew intuitively.

First, he orchestrated a cue. A prompt.

> "For years, people had felt a film on their teeth and had never worried about it, and you don't need toothpaste to get rid of it," Charles Duhigg says in his book, *The Power of Habit.* "But Hopkins drew people's attention to it by creating posters that read, "Get rid of that film. Pepsodent gives you a beautiful smile."

The cue Hopkins used to sell his toothpaste was the filmy plaque that forms naturally on teeth. But this was not enough to start a tooth-brushing habit in an entire nation. It also needed a reward. Here, it was the tingling, clean feeling you get after brushing your teeth. When consumers did not brush their teeth, they missed that feeling. The scientific power lies in the automatic brain response—whenever it now sees the cue (toothpaste), it craves the reward (tingling feeling).

It's not that others haven't tried selling Pepsodent before Hopkins. We all know that brushing our teeth is very important, right? But appealing to reason is a vain undertaking in brain science. We know that exercise and healthy food benefits us. We all know that we shouldn't binge this Netflix series but read this instructional book. But why do we still chose the former? Because our brain craves the reward it gets from an entertaining series rather than an instructional boring book. The reward we feel at eating a yummy burger rather than a salad. The reward we feel when we update the social media feed just like a Vegas slot machine, waiting if something good will appear.

Is there anything we can do to control our response? Yes. But not by willpower. Every time the new year hits, we think that by willpower alone we can stick to our resolutions. Anyone who has ever tried that will know the result. Instead, we have to trick our brain. The things we want need to become

- obvious
- attractive
- easy
- satisfying

For that, let's take a look at the Habit Loop, a neurological response that Charles Duhigg has defined in his book *The Power of Habit*.

The Habit Loop

According to Duhigg, the Habit Loop comprises four steps:

The Craving and the Response can also be summed up into the habit "Routine". To illustrate this further, here are some examples:

The cue to an exercise habit is putting on the running shoes. The craving for the endorphin rush and the feeling of accomplishment settles in. The response is the workout itself, and the reward is the high feeling afterwards.

Or the cue can be the buzzing of the phone, the craving for distraction, the opening of the new messages the response, and the reward the sense of connection, distraction and importance.

In “Atomic Habits”, James Clear defines the stages a little differently:

1. *Make it obvious*
2. *Make it attractive*
3. *Make it easy*
4. *Make it satisfying*

Let’s examine these four stages in a more artistic way.

#1 Cue: Make it obvious

The cue will tell you that your creative habit is about to start. We will go deeper in all the possibilities you have in terms of cues in the next chapter, because getting this one right is very important. The cue can vary from person to person, but it needs to suggest something pleasant, something that awakes your creative muse. Pull from your own nature and your happiest childhood memories, the things that set you at ease and give you a sense of safety and wonder.

#2 Craving: Make if attractive

The craving is always the desire to change the internal state. We don’t crave the TV but the relaxation it provides. We don’t crave the cigarette, but the relief it provides. Your creative habit should be attractive. The problem is: artists struggle with imposter syndrome and their own insecurities every time they stare at the blank canvas.

Decide in advance about your own nature and accept that you are an artist. You are creative. You have something to offer to this world.

The creative habit needs to be free from expectation. This moment is all about the creative outlet. Work hard to shut down your inner critic at this stage and allow the child to play instead. Nobody's watching. This is your own very personal space. Especially in the beginning, there will be resistance instead of craving, because you must experience the rush of deep work, a finished project and the satisfaction it will give you. In the beginning, there's only you and the hard labor of creative work. But there are small hacks that can make it attractive, which we'll talk about in the next chapters.

#3 Response: Make it easy

The actual creation process is the response, and you need to make it as easy as possible by having a plan. When you sit down at the desk or enter your studio, you need to answer the question: *What's next?*

This requires preparation. You need to think about the routine that will occur in the creative space, and contrary to assumption, exactly this routine will help you get over creative blocks and the fears that accompany every creative endeavor. How to create that plan to get the most artistic output in the shortest amount of time and produce your best work—we'll talk about this is detail.

#4 Reward: Make it satisfying

Scientifically, the reward is the purpose of every habit and thus a very important part of the habit loop. This reward initially motivates us in the first place and is—surprise, surprise—anything that produces a positive emotion. Contentment, relief, pleasure, relaxation. Your mind is constantly analyzing the environment for hints of where rewards could be located. If you train your brain to associate the cue with the reward, it will automatically respond to the cue with the routine—the craving and response. The challenge is to create a habit that leads to a satisfying and positive emotion, a lot of which can be achieved by a shutdown ritual and some tracking metrics.

So these are the four steps. If any of those are missing, the habit loop won't occur. It's important to know and understand the theory behind habit formation before we jump into the practicalities. The genuine challenge in forming a creative habit is that it needs to be addressed differently than forming an exercise habit for example, because it needs to deliver a framework for your inner creative child to emerge and help you produce your best work. That's why you need to recreate it from time to time. It will need change and novelty to keep the creativity going, and the moment you sense you've entered the comfort zone, you must evaluate whether you have to remove yourself from it. A little comfort is good, but too much of it can squander your creativity.

How, despite the automations, you can learn to engage the creativity inside, is an essential part of creative habit forming. The next chapters are all about finding the right things for you—your personality, your creative endeavors, and this particular season of your life. Be flexible with habits, and consult this book again and again for ideas on how to tweak and improve your creative habit, or maybe just give it a new spin. We will examine different writers and artists who had interesting habits, and the principles behind those habits to apply them to your life. Turn the page, and let's form a habit that will make an enormous difference in your happiness, your quality of life and the world around you with the work you create.

Triggers for Creatives

Friedrich Schiller was an 18th century German writer, a man with many professions—poet, philosopher, historian, playwright and physician—and a very peculiar habit. He's one of the most famous and respected members of Germany's literary elite until this date. I went to school in Germany, and we always read and marveled upon his works.

Schiller had a very unusual writing habit, and it speaks volumes about how habits can hack our brain. He used the odor of rotting peaches to get inspired. Just imagine it for a moment: he let some peaches or other fruit rot and used this smell strategically to inspire him to writing.

Why did this lunacy work? If you paid attention in the previous chapters, you know. There's no magic in rotting peaches. Nothing that the odor in itself holds to inspire. It functioned as a cue for Schiller's brain.

A cue is a small thing with a tremendous impact. It triggers the habit loop, giving your brain a signal and making sure you will see the habit through. But I'd like to propose an outrageous notion: if you pick the right cue, it can function as or at least support all four steps of the habit loop. A cue can be obvious, attractive, easy and satisfying.

Maybe not rotting peaches, mind you. And if you manage an ingenious combination of triggers that are right for your personality, you might hit the jackpot. Let me explain.

My go-to cue for creative writing time is as simple as it is powerful. It's my morning cup of coffee at my desk. It combines three different cues: time, place and another habit, offering me the benefit of a craving (I love excellent coffee), and supporting the sense of satisfaction (drinking it while I put words on paper).

Let's now look at four different types of cues that you can either combine or use separately to create an amazing entryway into your creative habit.

Cue #1: Time

Stephen King has many secrets. One of them is his routine. Here's how's he describes it:

> "I have a glass of water or a cup of tea. There's a certain time I sit down, from 8:00 to 8:30, somewhere within that half hour every morning."

I love the start of his writing time—at the center: **the morning**. Every morning. He doesn't have a rigid time, just around half an hour when he writes. Writing in the morning is key for Stephen King, as it is for countless other artists.

Why mornings?

Scientists have proven that during the morning hours, our subconscious is more active while in the evening, the conscious takes over. Deriving from your subconscious can have amazing effects on your creativity. You come up with new ideas, unforeseen twists and solutions to problems that you wouldn't have discovered in the evenings. Your subconscious is free to work and flourish. It can give you fresh ideas. And make your work more creative and more original.

In the morning, you have more energy.

If you have a day job, creating after you come home from work is an impossible task. You're exhausted from the day. You still have to do chores at home and all you want is some relaxation. Whereas in the morning, you're still full of energy to do artistic work.

I love how Stephen King begins his ritual with a glass of water or a cup of tea. It's not incidental. Hydrating yourself in the morning is crucial. Do whatever you need to wake up; wash your face, drink water, brush your teeth. Then move straight into writing mode.

There's no disturbance.

Look at Hemingway's writing routine:

> "When I am working on a book or a story, I write every morning as soon after first light as possible. There is no one to disturb you and it is cool or cold and you come to your work and warm as you write."

It's a delight to do creative work in the morning when the world is still asleep or waking up, when there are no phone calls or emails competing for your attention, trying to distract you from the important task. It's much easier to focus in the mornings. No family members storming the room. No kids yelling and crying in the background. Just you and your story.

Many creatives don't consider themselves morning people. It's true that some people have more energy and stamina in the evening. Scientists call it chronotype, and it can shift over a person's lifetime. But even if you consider yourself an owl, a creative habit in the morning with all its advantages is still worth overcoming the chronotype. Don't give up before you try it for at least 1-2 weeks.

Barbara Kingsolver, Pulitzer Prize nominee, has written over a dozen books, the last nine of which have all made the New York

Times bestseller list. During a 2012 interview, she talked about her daily routine as a writer and a mother:

> "I tend to wake up very early. Too early. Four o'clock is standard. My morning begins with trying not to get up before the sun rises."

Ouch. It even hurts reading this. You don't have to go to such extremes. Start with waking up 20 minutes earlier than usual; five minutes to wake up, fifteen minutes to do your creative routine. Every morning. If you're up for it, you can still do more work in the evening, but try this small ritual during your mornings first. See what impact it has on your creativity, both quality and quantity.

If you can't establish a creative habit in the early mornings because it just doesn't fit into your life—your job starts in the middle of the night or you have to work very late, for example—this should not be an excuse to give up altogether.

> In the end, there is no ideal condition for creativity. What works for one person is useless for another. The only criterion is this: Make it easy on yourself. [...] All preferred working states, no matter how eccentric, have one thing in common: When you enter into them, they compel you to get started."
>
> Twyla Tharp, The Creative Habit

J. K. Rowling went to a coffee shop with her daughter after work to write because for her, it was the only feasible thing to do at that time. E. B. White never waits for ideal conditions. If the noise in his house becomes too much of a disturbance, he just picks another place where he can go. In his words, "a writer who waits for ideal conditions under which to work will die without putting a word on paper."

Maybe you can't even establish a set time where you can create every single day because your daily life is not structured. Don't wait for ideal conditions. If you can, pick a set time in your day. Preferably the morning. If not, just be spontaneous and pick a free time-window in your day, using the other cues to set off the habit loop.

Cue #2: Place

Our environment has a significant impact on us. Research shows that an adequate amount of light improves mood and energy levels, while poor lighting contributes to depression and other deficiencies in the body. The amount and type of lighting directly affect concentration, appetite, mood, and many other aspects of daily life. And while you cannot influence the weather and sunlight, you don't have to be a victim of your environment. Instead, use environment design to create the best possible space to trigger your habit.

George R. R. Martin writes in a cabin in New Mexico he calls "the bunker". Maya Angelou rents a special hotel room to write. For his breakthrough book *Carrie,* Stephen King would literally lock himself in the laundry room.

But you don't have to go to these lengths to establish your creative habit. After that laundry novel, King now sits in the same seat, and his papers are all arranged in the same places. Just having a place where you can return to, something that signals to the brain: this is my creative space, is enough.

To create an ideal environment, pull from your own nature and personality. Would you rather enjoy a cosy place laid out with blankets and candles? Or an industrial space that looks clean and minimalistic? Do you want your desk to be free of clutter, or do some books and paper where you can scribble ideas drive you towards production? What do you even work on? A canvas, a notebook (lined? blank?), a typewriter or a computer? Pull some inspiration from interior design books and Pinterest. Insert visual cues that set you at ease, give you a sense of wonder and safetyg. Your creative space should look inviting.

Key to environment design is also to reduce the friction, so it doesn't require a lot of willpower to start where you left off with the creative endeavor last night. If you create in the morning, make sure you set everything up the night before. Prepare everything in the best way possible so you can walk in and start. A beautiful and functional creative space will make it easy to get to the habit itself. Create a cocoon that will help you immerse yourself into the creative task and lure you in with an invitation you cannot decline.

Having said all this, you might not have the luxury to have a creative space of your own. Maybe you need to leave home to write, or you don't have a corner to spare in a tiny apartment. This should not stop you from creating content. Here's what writer David Baldacci has to say about that:

> "The place to write is in your head. I cocoon myself and I can write anywhere."

David Baldacci wrote his thrillers very late at night after a full day of work, or at his lunch hour. For years. He just had this inner compulsion to write and didn't focus so much on the where.

A dedicated special place can be a great cue for the creative habit. It can reduce friction and the inner resistance and make it much easier to establish this habit. If you can, find your perfect corner that will spark your creativity. If it's not possible, don't despair. The next cue is as powerful and you can utilize it in every situation.

Cue #3: Another Habit

American novelist Jack Kerouac established a ritual around his writing routine. He lit a candle and wrote by its light, and blew it out when he was done for the night. Why do rituals like this work? They have their root in the Diderot Effect, something initially connected to consumer behavior.

French philosopher Denis Diderot, originally poor, sold his personal library to Catherine the Great, Empress of Russia. With his new wealth, he bought a scarlet robe. But the robe was too beautiful to fit into the rest of his possessions. He upgraded. Decorated his home with expensive sculptures, a new table, a mirror. After him was named the effect that describes the tendency for one purchase to lead to another. If we obtain new possessions, it often leads to a spiral of consumption, which is inherent in the human tendency to perform actions in succession. You go to the bathroom, wash your hands, remember that you need fresh towels, walk to the laundry room and so on. Using this tendency is what James Clear calls "habit stacking", stating the following formula:

"After [CURRENT HABIT], I will [NEW HABIT]."

He gives the Diderot Effect a positive spin and suggests using the natural momentum of a behavior to get to the next one. It works especially well when you integrate it after a habit you already have in place (like my morning coffee, for example), and when the cue is "highly specific and immediately actionable". That's why lighting the candle worked well for Kerouac.

Stephen King always has a glass of water or a cup of tea and vitamin pills. These morning habits are stacked together with his writing habit. Right after he does this, he sits down to write. These small habits can serve as very effective triggers, especially because the creative habit itself seems too overwhelming. Writing an entire book? Creating a YouTube channel? Setting up a blog? If a small, specific and easy habit precedes, it's easy to trick your brain into the next daunting task. Start with a cup of coffee (French press, porta filter coffee machine or AirPress), a cup of tea or water—something that is easy and enjoyable. It will take time, but after a while of persistent stacking, your brain will connect the dots automatically.

Cue #4: Accountability

I love challenging myself. No-one else needs to be involved. I love setting goals: how many words I want to write daily or how many times I want to work out weekly. This is why I love being a solopreneur.

Not so much my husband. He recently embarked on a project

where he took two other people with him. They were doing Zoom calls every single night for hours to be accountable to each other and work alongside. While such a way to create would suffocate me, this collaboration fueled him to work harder, to show up every single day and to reach his goals.

All of us are wired differently. And for many people, accountability and collaboration are the most powerful tools to start a creative habit. If you're—like my husband—one of those people, you need accountability partners.

Even for me, a hopeless introvert who doesn't want anyone to be involved in her process (at least until a certain point), I often head out to a co-working space where I work alongside several freelance friends. We're not all writers. Everybody has their own project. But the fact that all of us sit down to do something in one room motivates me to get the work done and not wander into procrastination or distraction.

If you don't have anybody close who could become an accountability partner, find people online—in Facebook groups or forums. Just set up a goal to work at a certain time in the morning, all of you remotely from where you live. But you'll know: *people are working right now, I have to show responsibility and be accountable,* and it will help you concentrate on your task and don't skip the habit. Being accountable to others will pick you up on the days when you don't feel like creating or don't think you can make it. It will force you to abandon other plans.

Now take a step back.

Examine all three cues and pick those that fit your personality and your circumstances. Can you pick a set time of the day? A certain place that you can design? Can you pair it with another habit that is already in place? Can you take people alongside for accountability? Remember: the key lies in simplicity. In the fact that you want to make the process as frictionless as possible to avoid overthinking, give yourself time to fight this inside battle and fall into procrastination.

Can you pick a habit that combines the best of all (or at least most) worlds? My morning coffee has worked wonders for me. It combines a habit already in place with a time and a location (my desk). All of these together are a ritual—a cue for my brain that the creative habit is about to begin. The reward is the yummy coffee, the cozy place at my desk aligned with candles and small lights, the early calm and solitude of the morning, the feeling of satisfaction as the blank page is inhabited with words… all of this is the perfect basis for a creative habit. For me. But you have to look at yourself and find what's ideal for your personality and your circumstances.

Don't be afraid to try things out. Don't be afraid to fail if you made sure you gave it a solid couple of weeks. Don't even be afraid to alter a year-long habit if the season of your life has changed, and it doesn't work for you anymore. The creative habit is organic. Beautiful and empowering. And once you establish it, you won't remember life without it.

But wait a minute… what now? You've created your ideal place and your special beverage, maybe some odor of rotting peaches, and now you're wondering what to do. Where to start. To make sure you see the habit through, you absolutely need to have a clear and structured process.

The Battle Plan

Busy, busy, busy. This is what most of our days look like. We run from one errand to another. But do we produce work of value? Have we accomplished something that matters in the long run? For most of our tasks, the answer is no. We're just busy putting out fires.

The only way to produce meaningful creative work is what Georgetown University computer science professor Cal Newport calls "Deep Work". Newport writes that deep work is, "professional activity performed in a state of distraction-free concentration that push your cognitive capabilities to their limit. These efforts create new value, improve your skill, and are hard to replicate." Creativity, in order to be valuable, original and powerful, has to come from deep work. Deep work requires laser-like focus in a world where we're expected to be online and accessible all the time. It requires dedication, a plan, and training—like a muscle that has to be built.

Your creative time therefore has to be sacred. A cocoon where nothing can get in, especially no external triggers that will distract you. Distraction is a terrible enemy. According to a University of California Irvine study, "it takes an average of 23 minutes and 15 seconds to get back to the task." So before we jump into the battle plan for your creative routine, we need to talk about external triggers first.

External triggers

Pong.

My eyes slide over to the phone next to my laptop. I read the notification. Nothing major. They switch back. In this one second, my focus is gone. My attention has shifted, and it's getting harder and harder to get back to the work I'm committed to.

As a writer, I struggled to get words on paper because the pings and pongs of everyday life constantly distracted me. It's not only the phone, it can be family members or colleagues walking in, an email notification sliding into my peripheral vision. I always wear headphones when I write. They help me block out the noise of a distracting environment. But they can't help with the "urgent" requests that come in every five minutes.

> "Today, much of our struggle with distraction is a struggle with external triggers."
>
> Nir Eyal, Indistractable

Deep Work is always a target. Internal triggers can be an immense problem, especially when we have unsolved issues and are amid a personal crisis. But external distraction lurks around every corner. External triggers have become a real problem in this modern age—because of the mobile phone, but also because of the culture. People expect us to present, to answer their requests in every living moment.

We want everything *now*. We want the answer now. We want people to reply to our emails and requests and meetings now. But productivity and deep work that leads to meaningful results takes a tall. We've been sitting at the desk for eight straight hours, or more, but somehow haven't got anything done.

Why is this? Researchers have found that when people are interrupted during a task, they subsequently make up for lost time by working faster, but the cost is higher levels of stress and frustration. By responding to everything, we condition our brain to respond instantly and thus lose the ability to do deep work. It's a skill. The more we jump from one task to the other and answer to all the distractions competing for our attention, the more we lose the ability to do deep and meaningful work.

Can't we just ignore the notifications that pop up and the people that want our attention? A study published in the Journal of Experimental Psychology: Human Perception and Performance found that receiving a cell phone notification but not replying to it was just as distracting as responding to a message or call. You don't even have to respond to the notification. The disruption is enough to distract you.

Not all external triggers are evil, though. Studies have found that motivational messages help smokers quit. If we receive good news and motivational messages, they can help us to get through the day. This is where accountability partners come in handy. But how can we separate the good triggers from the bad ones, and how can we get rid of this constant distraction that prevents us from the good and deep work of raw creativity?

The simple and secret method lies in answering a critical question: **Is this trigger serving me or am I serving it?** The problem is: 90% of our triggers turn us into slaves. We become slaves of our environment, slaves of our phone, slaves of our desktop and email programs. We cannot escape it, cannot outwit them. They are programmed to trick our brains into dependancy. They are not serving us anymore. We are serving them. If you want to reclaim your freedom again, perform deep and creative work, you need to eliminate external triggers altogether during your creative time.

#1 Get a brightly colored vest.

Hospitals US-wide suffer from extra costs of $3.5 billion in medical expenses because of human error. Most of those result from distracting external triggers that prevent highly trained, very well-intentioned people to focus on their task. Studies found that nurses experienced 5-10 interruptions each time they dispensed medications.

Becky Richards developed a solution, one that was not met with enthusiasm from her nursing colleagues. She proposed that they wear brightly colored vests to let others know that they were dispensing medication and should not be interrupted. The nurses did not like being on display like this, and the idea nearly failed. Until the hospital administration provided Becky Richards with the results of her experiment four month later: there was a 47% drop in errors.

If you want to focus, you need a brightly colored vest. Not literally, of course, but you need something to let the others know that you cannot be disturbed. In *Indistractable,* Nir Eyal proposes a big card with a large font placed on your computer monitor or on your desk that says: *I need to focus right now, but please come back soon*. A card that lets people around you know that you don't want to be interrupted. One that sends a very unambiguous and clear message.

There are more radical approaches. You could wear flickering lights on your head to let everybody else know you're in focus mode right now. Or go with something less glamorous and put up a sign on your office door. Communicate with your family if you're working from home. Express that the work you're doing is important and you need undisrupted time.

A neat side effect: accountability. You put up a sign for everybody else to see. You tell people you're going to do the work, and you feel extra pressure to get it done because you said so. This pressure motivates you to not be distracted and do focused work.

#2 Why a radical approach to the phone is vital

For six hours a day, his phone is on flight mode. This is what a friend of mine does for productivity. And while this might not be right for everybody, there are still radical things that you need to do in order to hack back your phone.

The best way to go is to turn the phone on flight mode. Put it away altogether during creative time, if possible. If you absolutely need it, turn off notifications. All of them. But what if there is an emergency? What if people need me? The problem with today's communication is that people write messages all the time. You'd be surprised how rare it is that they actually pick up the phone and dial your number. Trust me on that: if there is an emergency, they will call. Twice, if necessary. Also, many requests resolve themselves if you just add time to the equation.

#3 The psychological effects of a cluttered desktop

A study by researchers at Princeton University found that people performed poorly on cognitive tasks when objects in their field of vision were in disarray as opposed to neatly arranged. The same effect applies to digital environments, according to a study published in the academic journal Behaviour & Information Technology.

A cluttered desktop has devastating psychological effects on your performance. If you want to be productive, you need to bring order to the chaos. If you don't have the time and motivation to do so, I'll give you a simple hack that will once and forever remove the clutter from your desktop. Admittedly, I stole it from Nir Eyal. But why not spread genius ideas?

Create a folder on your desktop and name it "EVERYTHING". Select every file and put it into the folder. That's it. As if stuffing all the chaos into a cupboard. Of course, it's more helpful if you can get rid of old files and sort through the mess.

But if you just don't have the time and energy, use the simple hack to clean your desktop. This will enhance your productivity and give you calm once you open your computer to do creative work (if this is how you create content).

Also, and this is key, turn off all desktop notifications. Because if something jumps into your field of vision while you're working, it will instantly distract you.

. . .

Controlling external triggers has not only helped me become more productive during the time I dedicate to creative work, but it has given me back peace and calm in general because my notifications are off even when I do not work. This helps me connect with my family, friends, and focus on the surroundings. It frees me to focus on my environment and just let my thoughts float to generate new ideas and observe the world, which is so vital for us creatives.

External triggers influence not only our work performance. They influence our entire lives. Remember the critical question I proposed in the beginning of this chapter: **Is this external trigger serving me or am I serving it?** We can't have any external triggers during our creative work. But even in general, as you go about your day (because creativity is part of your daily life), pay attention to external triggers. Stop serving them, allow more time for daydreaming and lingering, and take back control of your day.

Your creative habit routine

"If you don't know where you are going, you'll end up someplace else."

Yogi Berra, former New York Yankees catcher

When I decided that I wanted to write my first novel, I struggled for almost a year. Sat down in front of that blank page. Wrote some sentences. Maybe a paragraph or two. Read it again. Rewrote it. But I just couldn't continue. So I began to dread the writing time and find excuses to skip it. Luckily, the inner compulsion wouldn't let go.

Creatives find themselves before blockages more often than all other professions. I'm certain that you've hit a wall more than once. That you've experienced this famous term coined "writer's block" or any other block that prevented you from creating content. Why is that?

I'd like to propose an outrageous notion. It's because you lack a plan. It's because when you look at this blank canvas, your blank screen, or your white sheet, it scares you to death and you don't know what to do next. The good thing is: you can change it. You can come up with a plan—a structure for your creative work that will help your creativity flourish more than it will strangle it.

Dr. Seuss wrote his book "Green Eggs and A Ham" on a bet that he couldn't write a book with 50 or fewer distinct words. He won the bet and produced one of his most popular works. His first successful children's book was also the result of a challenge to write a book in under a certain number of words. You see, creativity flourishes with the right restrictions and the right structure. Because if you give it a direction, if you give it a challenge, then you rid it of the uncertainty of the blank canvas. With a creative routine or a creative plan, you need to come up with something that is efficient for you. Something that gives you enough structure and challenge, but at the same time doesn't strangle your creativity.

How to structure your creative time

Step #1: Plan the entire process

First, consider the big picture. Most of the time, our creative endeavors require a lot of time and dedication, and scare us because of their enormity. Writing a book? A whole novel? It seems near to impossible.

So in order to help yourself, you need to break down this endeavor into smaller steps. For example: starting with a rough outline, then moving on to creating the characters and character sheets, then the first draft process, reading and editing, the first print run, and so on.

You can structure every creative process into action steps. "Writing a novel" is far too abstract. When you write down these steps, they need to be concrete, clear and simple. If you don't know how to do them, research it first. For example, if I want to create my characters, I first need to come up with a process for it. I might write down some questions I need to answer, come up with character sheet templates I want to work with.

Split your creative endeavor into actionable steps and think about every single step in detail so that when you embark on the journey, you know exactly what to do.

Step #2: The imagination exercise

When you sit down at the beginning of your creative routine, decide what you want to do in this session. Look at your overall plan. See where you're at, what you've accomplished so far. Then close your eyes. For several seconds, just imagine what you're about to do. Imagine the scene you're about to write, the smells, the sounds, how it looks, how the characters look. Or imagine the piece of content you're about to plan out, how you want this YouTube video to look or this email to start.

Just give the brain some time to process what you're about to do and let it imagine the whole thing before you do it. This is insanely helpful because it will direct your brain towards the creative task. It doesn't have to be long. It can be 10 or 30 seconds. Just breathe, close your eyes and imagine it—these couple of seconds are a well of inspiration and motivation.

Step #3: Use time blocks

Because you're aiming for deep undistracted work, start with short time blocks. If you haven't been practicing deep work before, this will help you succeed. Our brain is used to giving in to distractions all the time. It's difficult to focus on one single task in the beginning. So just give it a test run and start with five minutes of deep dedicated work with no distraction. If you see that you can continue, increase the time to 10 minutes or 15 minutes. I'd say the maximum is around 20 to 30 minutes.

Take a quick break, drink some water, walk around, and then start another time block. This is also called the Pomodoro technique, and you can use timers to help you get through these bursts of work. What these timers do though is help you focus on deep work and push away every distracting thought to later. You can glance at your timer and tell yourself: *Okay, I have 10 minutes left. After those 10 minutes, I can still get to this distraction and follow up on this thought and this idea, or at least write it down.* The distraction might be gone after 10 minutes, but the fact that you don't postpone it indefinitely provides you with peace of mind and helps push the distraction away more easily.

When the time block starts, know precisely what you want to do during this time—write, brainstorm, sketch, research, and so on. This is why the imagination exercise is so helpful. It focuses your brain on the task ahead and helps you get the most of the time block.

Flow state is addictive, and you can train it like a muscle. If you establish a daily creative habit, you muscle of doing deep work and getting into the state of flow will become stronger, and you will see how you will produce better and better work in shorter amounts of time. Don't rigidly stick to the time sprints. When I'm writing a chapter, am in a flow state and the timer runs down, I still continue to write. I use the momentum. The timer helps avoid procrastination and build momentum. When you're in flow state already, you can ignore the timer and continue your work.

During those time blocks, allow yourself to play, go through scenarios and also make mistakes. If you come up with some creative idea that doesn't fit into your plan, just go with it, try it. Allow yourself to make mistakes as long as you stick to your creative project. For example, if you're writing an email and you think, I'd like to include a chart or an image, give yourself permission to do that. After the clock has run down and you finish your dedicated time of focus, use the next time block to find a good image or create a graphic for your content.

Remember, this is your creative time. You're allowed to create and to experiment. You're allowed to do things you like, to play and get into the zone.

Step #4: Set goals and track your progress

Always set goals for your creative time. For example, if you're a writer, set a goal for a word count. It can be anything you can measure your success with. This small amount of stress helps you focus and achieve one certain goal, and will also ensure you can come up with great ideas in a short amount of time. Research has proven that small doses of stress are helpful for idea generation and finding solutions to problems.

Don't wear yourself down but make room for improvement. Start out with smaller goals. And as you build your creative muscle, increase them. We often either underestimate or overestimate what we can do in a certain timeframe. But as you continue to do these time sprints, you will inevitably notice how you get better.

At the end of your creative session, always track what you have accomplished, some goal you set in advance—a finished blog post, one or two emails, three chapters. Write down what you have accomplished, or maybe what you haven't accomplished and need to do in the next session.

Accountability and the pleasure of accomplishment play a huge role here, whether you're accountable to yourself or to others. Measure progress honestly, be honest about what you can achieve and how you can improve. There's no point in cheating—this is for you and no one else. It serves to build your creative muscle.

Step #5: Write a note for the next day

When your creative time ends and you've achieved your goals, or at least managed to create some content, you'll be filled with energy and motivation. So make sure in the fifth step to write down everything you need to do in the next session. As you sit down or enter your creative studio on the next day, having these thoughts and this list of what to do next will help you start the flow state and get into the creativity mode quicker.

Hemingway, for example, never finished a chapter. He sometimes even left the sentences unfinished because when he sat down the next time, he could pick up from where he left off. I like leaving myself hints and thoughts about what to do next and how to continue the game plan, without wasting precious time to remember the last thing that was on my mind.

Now it's your turn. Sit down and write a creative plan for your habit. Go through all the five steps listed above and write a battle plan. The trick is to never, ever sit down in front of a blank page or a blank canvas. Always have something that prompts you to create and helps gain momentum.

Seven hacks to get out of a rut

Why are so many people exhausted? Surveys show that 77 percent of people experienced burnout somewhere in life. Why are people stressed to the point that their bodies suffer serious illness?

The world drains a well planted inside of us. Life becomes about results we have to deliver, chores we have to do. Economy needs us to function, thus draining our creativity through everyday life routine. There comes a point in our lives when we stop creative play. We fail to let our souls be free and create something meaningful. We are made to be creative. We need a creative outlet in order to thrive, in order to escape depression and burnout. But fostering this creative play is difficult because it requires intention.

And as much as you try to establish a habit, and trick your brain into the most frictionless process, this habit cannot become a cage for your creativity. In order to be a better creative, somebody who can escape burnout and stress, and at the same time create an extraordinary work that stands out, you have to do uncomfortable things. Break out from your routine once in a while, be alert about whether you lose the sense of play, fascination and happiness in your work.

Yes, we have to do the work. We have to show up every single day.

Sometimes we have to power through. But it doesn't mean that we have to be miserable. It doesn't mean that we have to imprison ourselves into the same old hamster wheel we fled in our day job. The beauty about creativity is that you can foster it. But this requires moving out of your comfort zone. It requires intentional effort all the time. The steps can be drastic. They can be small. What you need to do is tweak and change your creative routine once in a while to bring back the enthusiasm that you felt the first time you sat down to do this project.

The process of writing a first draft demands a lot from me, but I'm not content with just resigning and powering through. Instead, I look for ways to make this process more creative, more interesting for me, for example by dictating. Because I know when I rediscover my enthusiasm, my work will shine and be the best it can be.

There are some adjustments you make in order to change up your creative routine and bring out the best in you, bring back the inner child. I list them in no particular order, but I'll start with the most extreme one.

1. Empathy

I tell the story a lot in my emails. And if you are a subscriber, you probably know it, but bear with me for the sake of those who don't. In film school, a friend of mine wanted to shoot a short film about a homeless person. When he set out to write the script, he realized that he knew nothing about what it means to be homeless. Of course, he could do research. But what he did instead blew my mind. I don't know if I would have been brave enough for this. For one night, he became a homeless person himself. He spent a night on the streets in order to see what it feels like to be homeless. According to him, this was one of the most frightening and most life-changing nights of his life.

Sometimes theory is not enough. We can do research. We can read all kinds of articles, book, watch videos. But nothing beats experiencing those things firsthand. Writer David Baldacci has fired every single weapon there is. He could have researched it. He could have watched videos. But in his masterclass, he explains that he wanted to know what it feels like to shoot from this specific firearm. So when he writes about it, he describes not only the superficial technicalities, but the authentic feeling.

Empathy is a powerful weapon for a creative person. We have to get into the shoes of the people, get an appreciation for them. Try things we would have never tried before. You don't have to go to extremes, they can become dangerous. And maybe it's not a good idea to spend the night on the street as a woman. And maybe it's mentally critical when you're playing the Joker to lock yourself alone in a hotel room for weeks and stare at a blank wall.

We can still do uncomfortable things that do not endanger our lives or our wellbeing. We can test fire weapons in a safe environment. We can meet people and ask uncomfortable questions. We can take classes. We can travel. We can build experiences because experience, not theory, is what will make us grow as creatives. And those experiences will fuel us up to let our creativity grow, bring our content on a new level, feel what it means to be human in more depth. It will make you a better creative and it will drag you out of the ordinary.

2. Transfer your creative habit into another place.

If you're hitting a wall creatively and you don't need particular equipment for work, you could try to transfer your habit into another place, further away from the usual space. For example, go to a coffee shop, visit a library. Change up the scenery in any way possible.

Some people like to create outside, they go into the woods or sit down in their garden. Just once in a while, if you can try different places for your creation, you will see how it will fuel you up to work and will help you grow and rediscover the enthusiasm and the fun in work.

3. Do workations

Many creative people have adapted the value of workations.

Workstations are nothing else but short staycations where you just travel to another place, book a hotel or apartment in a place you like, and do the work. For example, if you're setting out to write a book, you could book a weekend or 3-4 days in a hotel somewhere further away and dedicate all of your time to writing this book.

Research travel is another great way to do workstations because they take you out of your original routine and force you to inhale the places and look at your project in a different light. You still focus on your project because you do research for it, but it deepens the understanding of what you're about to do. And it provides you countless great ideas.

When I wrote my first novel, I finished the first draft and did an editing round, but I still felt that something was missing. So I set out for five days to follow the route of my main character in the book—from the Highlands of Scotland down to London. It was such a glorious trip, not only because I love Scotland. It changed my book in many ways, gave me entirely new ideas, provided me with inspiration and fueled me with even more passion to finish the story and to publish it.

4. Change tiny things in your environment

If you work alone, work in a co-working space instead. If you've always worked surrounded by others, try to work alone. Change the space you're working in by buying a new desk. Insert a workout in between breaks, or change the scent of the candle you always light. Try changing up smaller things, because often, this might be just enough. Even these small things might fuel you with fresh energy and new passion for your project and take you out of the soul drenching routine.

5. Do free writing.

In the book "The Artist's Way", Julia Cameron proposes the idea of Morning Pages. Every morning, you sit down and write several pages of free writing. Whatever comes to mind. Many creatives have described the Morning Pages as life changing.

Even if you're not a writer, free writing can alter everything. It provides you with headspace to generate original ideas. Freewriting can be scary, especially in the beginning, because you just don't know what to write. But as you push on, a well of possibilities opens up.

Don't censor yourself. Nobody sees it. This is your time. And if you try free writing for a while, you will see how it will reveal things about who you are, about where you're stuck, and about the solutions to creative problems.

6. Produce different content

If you're in a rut and your habit has become annoying, a burden, try to do a different type of content. If you're a novel writer, shoot a video, do photography, start a podcast. Sometimes, these new skills and types of content will teach you new things about creativity, and about yourself. They will splash more creative energy in your face to go back to your original content and become more passionate about it.

Again, don't be afraid to try new things. If you're tired of shooting videos, write a book. If you're tired of writing books, start a podcast. You will see how these different types of content will help you rediscover the creative spark.

7. Find a tribe

When in film school, we often sat down at the pub near the university grounds in the evenings, and talked about all kinds of movies, projects, and ideas. These discussions fueled my passion and awoke the childlike sense of wonder.

Talk to people who are passionate about the same things that you are, but maybe have different outlooks on them. It's so rewarding to talk about ideas and projects and see what others have to say about your creative work, because they might have different, but very interesting ideas that give you a spark. This is the beauty of a film school, and even as I write this, nostalgia fills me. Now that I work alone, I don't have this luxury. And probably you don't, either.

Try at least once a year to visit a conference of like-minded people in person and make connections. And if you have people around you that are creative, forge friendships, gather regularly. This exchange of ideas will fuel you, and you'll feed off each other's energy.

These are my seven hacks to stay alert and grow creatively. Be very mindful about whether you've reached a comfort zone that drenches your creativity. Sometimes a comfort zone can come in handy because you know what you're doing and you get into the state of flow, but other times a comfort zone can become a prison.

Walk the balance. Regularly change things up to spice up your creative routine.

PART III

Business

A story is meant to be read, seen and connected with. Otherwise, it's meaningless. There are countless stories out there. Powerful stories. Ones that have the potential to make a great impact. Yet nobody knows about them. One of those was the diary of Eva Heyman who chronicled her daily life before and after the 1944 German invasion of Hungary. It began with her 13th birthday and ended on 30 May 1944, just days before her deportation to Auschwitz, where she died on 17 October 1944. Her story was long forgotten. But through a unique form of marketing, this story impacted millions of people, forged connections and changed the way people saw the world.

The project was called Eva Stories: a campaign that chronicled the last days of Eva in 1944 through Instagram Stories. Eva Stories generated a lot of controversy prior to its launch on Israel's Holocaust Memorial Day, with critics claiming it was in bad taste. But this controversy helped the @Eva.Stories Instagram account amass over 180,000 followers even before the series debuted, and when it did, it became an international phenomenon overnight. Across 70 Instagram Stories chapters, the film received more than 300 million views in less than 48 hours—coming from across the globe, despite the campaign being focused on an Israeli audience.

The stories were created to be interactive, to provide an experience. Eva used Instagram Stories' questions feature to ask questions such as how to cheer up her grandfather or get the boy she likes to notice her. The initiators were the 56-year-old tech and media billionaire Mati Kochavi and his daughter Maya, founder of the popular tween platform StelloGirls. "We got such a crazy amount of engagement from that and realized how connected people were to the story," Maya told in an interview.

At the end, a challenge was posed to viewers: "Write a message in memory of Eva." Within a few minutes, thousands of messages flooded in. "We will always love you and remember you," one user wrote.

This example illustrates the power of creativity combined with marketing. The story of Eva was always there. Written for everybody to read. Like your creative projects, whether they are still in your head, on a piece of paper, or maybe lost somewhere in the depth of the internet where nobody can find them. Without marketing, they remain unseen, unread, and useless. They forge no connection. They have no audience. And thus, they die.

I realize that it's a harsh statement. But look at it from a different angle. With the right marketing tools, a story can be brought to life so much that it connects to millions of people. This is the possibility in this day and age. The example of Eva Stories also illustrates how profoundly creative marketing is, and how much courage and love it demands—to go up against criticism, to make something that daring, and to trust that the right people will connect with the message.

Therefore, I couldn't write a book about creativity without bringing in business. Both are different ends of the same rope. Only in the balance they bring forth something living and breathing that can change the world. Most creative people shy away from the word "business". They don't want to run a business. They don't want to do marketing. *Can't somebody else do the marketing for me?* I know you've asked that question, at least in secret. Because I have.

But if you want to become a better creative and storyteller, read on, because this is about to change your life. In this part of the book, you'll learn:

- what misconceptions are holding you back and how you can reframe them
- the two ways of combining business and creativity
- the three steps needed to perform daily for a successful creative business
- the three parts of a creative business plan and how to write the one that fits your needs

As always, we need to start with mindset. Because like the roots that provide a tree with energy and fuel, so is the mindset that serves as an invisible foundation for a fruitful creative business.

Lies you believed

"I'm a creative, not a businesswoman."

This was my opinion of myself. All I wanted was to write great stories. When I took the route of self-publishing (for financial reasons plus the freedom and control it provides), I knew I had to do the marketing part. I knew I had to run a business. Emphasis on *had* to.

Being a creative who fought her way to a degree in Engineering, I learned how to approach challenges. I educated myself: read many books on how to run a business, listened to podcasts, took several courses. And I still failed. My first book release was a disaster: my work swallowed by the dark forest of countless Amazon books, never to return.

After the initial setback, some mood swings and I-will-never-make-its combined with comfort food, I began to analyze: Why? How come I was familiar with the theory, and it did not work out? It all came back to my deep-seated, but deadly wrong opinion: *I'm a creative, not a businesswoman*. Of course, I had to do the marketing. But I regarded marketing as the "necessary evil". Deep down, I resented it.

If you feel the same way, you need to bust some misconceptions about business right now. This will change your approach, as it did for me, because those myths are holding you back in becoming a successful and prolific creative.

> "Our beliefs about what we are and what we can be precisely determine what we can be."
>
> Tony Robbins

This is true in every area of life—especially in business. The way you think about it will determine your results.

1. The Salesman Paradigm

Knock knock.

Behind the door awaits the sleazy salesman, trying to charm his way into your living room and your wallet. Sell a product with false embellishments to get his commission. Is this how you feel when you try to market your creative product? Like the dirty door-to-door salesman, convincing your email list and everybody else that your creation it worth their money?

A salesman's job is to trick the people into something they don't need. But your job is to find those who are desperate for what you offer. That's why it's so important to target your audience with knife-like precision. You're not marketing to everybody. You're not knocking on every door. And you're not selling a redundant product.

First, face the hard truth that your product might not be for your friends, colleagues, kids or spouse. You want the right audience, those who have been craving your product because it will solve their problem.

Second, you want to provide your audience with true value. If the product you deliver is something that will blow them off their feet, you can be proud to market it, sell it with integrity. And the result? They will thank you for it. They will rave about it in the reviews and recommend it to others.

You're not the door-to-door salesman because you are offering a valuable product to the right people, a product that will improve their lives, entertain them and give them what they have been craving.

2. The Sell-Below-Value Attitude

Giving away all your knowledge for free is like casting pearls before swine.

I'm not saying don't be generous. And giving away things for free is a great strategy to gain a following. But how much 'free' is too much? If you give people an extensive resource for free, containing all your knowledge, all your best content, the end-product's value will decrease in their eyes. This is just how we're wired. Don't be afraid to ask for money in exchange of your intellectual property. It's worth it if you put genuine effort inside.

As a teaser, you can give away a small amount of your knowledge or content for free, tease a little for those who want more. Sell the rest. If people enjoyed your free resource, they will gladly pay to dive deeper.

But what is the right price to set? A good rule of thumb is: Always price slightly higher than you are comfortable with. This will show that your product is premium and high-quality, and attach those who are interested in it. Aim for the top 10% of your market—or higher.

3. The Strategy Overwhelm

Metadata, retailers, SEO, paid advertising, newsletter swaps, give-aways, packaging, cash-flow, business plan… where to even start? You are bombarded with all kinds of different strategies. This overwhelm is what scares away the already shy business woman or man inside.

The first thing you need to do: bring order to the chaos. Give meaning to all those outlandish words that only seem scary because you don't know what's hidden inside. Educate yourself, at least to the extent necessary. That's why you bought this book. Once you label and understand the terms, you will master them. Write your own business plan and marketing strategy (more on that in the following chapters). Also, don't be afraid of trial and error when in comes to marketing. This is a game of testing. But that's also what makes it so much fun!

4. The Starving Artist Mindset

> "The writer must earn money in order to be able to live and to write, but he must by no means live and write for the purpose of making money."
>
> Karl Marx

It has become a badge of honor—the starvation and loneliness of an unacknowledged artist. He is too great to be recognized in his lifetime for the genius that he is. Aren't these the stories we tell ourselves? And the stories others tell us? Artists can't make any money. When I told my family I wanted to become an author, my parents watched me with bewilderment, and a dash of pity, asking if I shouldn't get "a real job". I don't blame them. This is the take society has on artists. That their work is not work at all. That they don't labor. That they are poor and that honestly, creativity is only a hobby. It's a great hobby, but please, also get a proper job. One that pays the bills.

What's the result? We feel bad to charge appropriately for our art. I can't tell you how often in the film industry I was asked to work "for credits". Would any plumber ever work for credits? Would any lawyer? Yet somehow, this is accepted in the creative industry. Although any artist knows that his work is as much craft, technique and time as any other, sometimes even more, because it requires not only your handiwork but your heart and soul. We still buy into that lie. We still work for free, undercharge, let us guilt ourselves into undervaluing our work and accept the fact that artists are supposed to be poor.

Yet reality looks different. Artists like Damien Hirst and J. K. Rowling are worth millions of Dollars. But you don't have to look that far. There are thousands of niche artists—independent musicians, writers, YouTubers, designers—who make more than a decent living without being all over the news. With the power of the internet, you just need your 1000 true fans to make a living from your art.

I've never heard of Joanna Penn until I became interested in self-publishing. She's not on TV and her books are not being made into movies. Yet not only was she able to quit her day job, but her husband could also quit his to help her with her business as a self-published author.

Yes, you need a set of skills and experience to make a decent amount of money. It takes time and practice. But what job doesn't? Every career has an entry level. The bonus about this one is: you get to do what you love AND make money.

5. The "Business-is-not-creative" Myth

I have a Bachelor of Engineering degree in Media Technologies. Let me tell you one thing—I'm not an engineer. I fought my way through physics, electro technology, signal theory and programming. It was the hardest degree I ever did. But by the end of the four years, I learned one thing—engineering can be highly creative. Because creativity requires problem solving in a unique way. A way nobody has thought of before. It requires connecting seemingly non-related notions and ideas, and forces to find a one-of-a-kind approach to a problem. So does engineering. What I took from this degree more than anything was the skill and persistence that is required to solve problems.

If engineering can be creative, so can business. It all depends on the way you approach it. Yes, business is about money, and numbers, and tracking and measuring. But it's also about people and connections and unique solutions to problems. Your customer's problems. Business requires you move from self-centered art to people-centred art. Business is a service.

You are forced to look at people's problems and find creative solutions for them. Solutions that nobody thought of before. Solutions neatly tied to your personality, your experience, and your uniqueness. Running a business is a creative endeavor and a lot of fun once you change your outlook on it. Yes, it's a different form of creativity. While pure art centers on itself and engineering centers on technology, business centers on people. Not on money. Not on scamming, as we established before. On the service to others. And this is a creative process.

The truths about creative business

Now that we've talked about the misconceptions, let's revisit some truths. These are the truths you need to instill into your belief system. It's hard because you've been preached quite the opposite for years on end. Depending on where you come from, some misconceptions are deeply rooted in your belief system while others are easy to get rid of. Revisit these truths time and time again until you adopt them to become your own. The way to run a successful creative business starts with your mindset.

You provide a solution for people's problems—be it entertainment, escape, inspiration or a how-to manual. You provide something that people are *actively* looking for. The power of a creative business is that this solution has the potential to take on a life of its own, helping people to reach goals and change lives.

An artist has the right to be paid because his work is worth it. People will gladly pay for your service or product because it's valuable. If you pour your soul and heart into the endeavor, and provide something unique, people will thank you for your work. Maybe you're not plumbing a toilet or operating on a liver, but your work is still craftsmanship that is worth its money.

. . .

Nobody will run your business for you. Nobody will do the marketing for you. As soon as you pay your taxes, you've got a business, whether you want it or not. Better embrace this fact and run a creative and innovative business. You are the best person to do it. Nobody will invest so much effort, thought and yes, creativity, into this business. It's as much a mirror of your own unique personality as is your creative work.

Marketing and business are fun and creative if—like your content—you view it as a story you want to tell. What is the story you want to tell people? The story has to be authentic. It has to mirror your beliefs, your personality, and the products you're offering.

Why there is no meaningful creativity without a business

This is a harsh statement. And by no means do I want to devalue all those artists who work hard and struggle to pay the bills or support themselves with a day job. But let me argue my point.

As mentioned before, business is, when done right, a service. It always has the customer in mind. It aims to provide value, solve a problem, and make lives better. Creativity has many forms. But if you want to create something meaningful, you have to turn away from yourself, your own expression of art, therapeutic means or "art for arts sake", and turn towards others. Ask yourself: how can the content I am creating benefit others, solve their problems? Think about why people should pay for your content. What are you providing them with? When combined with business, art goes from self-centered to people-centered.

Let me give an example. When I write my novel, it's only me at my desk, typing words unto the screen. It's a solo-show. And if that was it —me writing my novel and then moving on to the next—without marketing, without thinking about packaging and my readers and all the things business related, my work would be meaningless. Dead. Only in the interaction with readers, when I receive reviews, emails, calls, do I know how my work affected them. And can tweak it accordingly, make it more entertaining, more captivating for them. My work comes alive in the hands of readers. And because I do the marketing myself, because I run my business, I have the knowledge about what my readers need and what I can provide them with.

I solve *their* problem primarily, not mine.

A no less important side effect is that this feedback and this interaction motivates you to create more. It helps you to work without burning out. When your creativity lies dead in the corner and your words hit a wall without response, burnout is just around the block. But seeing the results—changed lives, money in your bank, feedback from your audience—makes an enormous difference in how long you can sustain your creativity and keep improving as an artist.

Reframe your thinking about business. It's not about scamming, making dirty money or devaluing your creativity. It's about people, about thriving and succeeding as an artist while you serve others.

Two ways to do creative business

There are two ways how creativity and business can coexist.

Everybody starts out with the first one. The second track takes time to build. Nobody can start from scratch with a huge backlist at their disposal. We all start from zero. The difference is that some people deliberately choose to stay on track one while others intend and manage to switch to track two. It all depends on your goals and/or comfort level with the risk track two entails.

Let's look at both of them in more detail.

Track #1: Support your creativity with a side track of commissioned work.

The Medici family, rulers and preeminent bankers of Florence primarily financed Michelangelo's work. They became his patrons from an early age, and they commissioned him to do work—contract work that Michelangelo regarded as a duty, not art. Ironically enough, these commissions produced some of Michelangelo's finest work, including the completion of the sculpture of Moses and the fresco covering the altar wall of the Sistine chapel.

Leonardo DaVinci also did a lot of commissioned work. For most of his life, he was in service of one great lord or another; he worked as a painter and sculptor in court, and he was an engineer. But this gave him time to work on his passion projects, like the Mona Lisa.

My own creative business stared the same way (not that I compare myself to Michelangelo or Da Vinci, mind you). I studied filmmaking. And while it's very hard to earn money when you're at the beginning of your writing career—they say you need at least 10 books to make a living—it's easier to get commissioned work as a freelance filmmaker. I worked for several companies, shot online advertising spots, edited news for TV stations. I did basically every job that helped me pay the bills while I focused on my creativity and my writing.

This is the first possibility for your business and your creativity to co-exist: you accept commissioned or freelance work, and at the same time, work on your passion projects. Some chose to continue on that road for years, and they enjoy it. I know a writer who edits the work of others and gets paid for this service. She loves to do both, and wouldn't dream of giving up the editing. She's happy with this arrangement, loves writing her books, but also enjoys doing commissioned work. It provides an additional safety net and is a nice break from the solo-creativity. And if that is a life you desire, try to find something that supports your creative endeavors seamlessly. Ideally it's not some mindless work like waiting tables at the restaurant all night, but something that has to do with your industry, something that connects you with the right people, and that helps you gain experience for your creative passion projects. This way, both tracks can coexist and support each other while you grow as a content creator.

And this can be the end of it. But some people are not content with this arrangement, for several reasons. They might not like commissioned work, they might not have enough time and/or headspace to do both. Some people crave the freedom disregarding the risk of having their creative business support them fully. And if you are one of them, like I am, this first track should flow into…

Track #2: Serve the market with your creative business.

A good friend of mine quit his law degree to become a blogger and copywriter. For the first years of his career, he worked for three days a week in an agency and wrote copy for them while for the rest of the week, he built his online business. But this was only the means to a goal. After a couple of years, when his business was making enough money, he quit his agency job and focused on that business solely: teaching others how to build a blog and a make money online.

Most of us, when we talk about "making our living with creativity" want both creativity and business to co-exist in the same space. This is possible, as countless creative entrepreneurs out there have proven. It just takes time, determination and resilience to get there. You will be able to support yourself and maybe even your family exclusively with your creative endeavors (meaning without commissioned work) —if you combine business and creativity. This is what I'll teach you in the next chapters.

And this won't necessarily mean that you will have less to do. It means you have more control, more time to devote to your business, and the freedom to focus on your creative work exclusively. To manage this, you will need to build a framework around your creativity. In the long run, you can't rely on one income stream. If, in this ever-changing world, this stream ceases to produce the usual results, your entire existence will crash.

For a sustainable creative business, you will need several streams of income. Streams that also will help you generate increasingly more passive income while you continue your work—for example books, courses, and other products that you can sell. This is your **backlist.** What you want for maximum security and outlook into the future is to gradually build a creative business with passive and active income streams flowing in every month.

To decide which path you want to take, know your ultimate goal. Why are you doing this? Do you want financial independence? Do you want to be a one person business, a solopreneur? Are you aiming for a big business with employees so you can outsource commissioned work, for example? Do you want to travel and live the nomad life? Or do you want to settle down and support your family?

Be very clear about what you want from your business. Revert to your Sweet Spot, your ideal daily life, and also your life's season. Do you want more time with your kids? Do you want to retire early and travel?

Also, keep in mind that your goals can change over time, but your Sweet Spot remains the same. What's your mission? What do you want from this endeavor? It forces you also to look at yourself as if looking in the mirror and asking: who am I? This is a process of discovery, not only of your creative business but also of your true self, because your Sweet Spot reflects who you truly are.

Not wanting to get too metaphorical or abstract, I just want to highlight the point that you need to know what you want from this before you start. Because if you don't, the waves and ever-changing trends of today's world might swoop over you and drown you. If you want to ride the waves instead, you need to know what you want from life, who you are, and what you want your business to look like.

In the next chapter, we will talk about how you can perform your business tasks daily and incorporate them into your daily life, much like the creative habit. Business and marketing have to be a daily effort and they have to go hand in hand with creativity.

Before we do that, answer the following questions:

- *What are your goals?*
- *What do you want from your creative business?*
- *What do you want your business to look like in the future (in 10 or twenty years)?*

These questions will help you navigate the changing seas of the creative business and get clarity about what you want to accomplish.

First, think about how you can combine commissioned work and build your backlist (track #1) in the most efficient way. Maybe become a coach, a virtual assistant or a freelance writer on the side while you work to write your books, build your YouTube channel or grow your mailing list? Be aware that this kind of freelance business won't run itself and will also need marketing efforts to attract clients. It even might be easier to keep a full or part-time day job.

If you intend to switch to track #2, ponder about the possibilities. Make a plan. And this is what we will do now, in the next chapters of the book.

Daily Business Practice

Novelist W. Somerset Maugham had miserable sales for his first novel, *Liza of Lambeth*. His publisher had no interest in advertising the book, which shouldn't come as a surprise. But Maugham didn't despair, concluding that he just had to talent. He took the matter in his own hands and placed a few classified ads in a few daily newspapers in London. The ads said:

"Young millionaire, lover of sports, cultivated, with a good taste of music and a patient and empathetic character wishes to marry any young and beautiful girl that resembles the heroine of W.S. Maugham's new novel."

Within 7 days, the first edition of his little known novel sold out. It got critical praise and popular sales.

This story proves that you are the best person to do your own marketing. Nobody cares about it as much as you do. Nobody puts as much effort and thought into it. And nobody will get on board with such bold and creative tactics. Don't you agree it was a brilliant move? And it worked. It kick-started Maugham's creative career.

It's no wonder that some experts say that 80% of your work should be marketing. I wouldn't go to these extremes, though. We are creatives, after all. We want to dedicate our primary work to craft. We want to dedicate our time to creating better things. Not only to marketing things that might not even be good enough. We want to become better content creators, better writers, YouTubers, filmmakers. We want our craft to shine and polish the work we do until it's the best it can be.

Still, I would go as far as saying: **you need to dedicate 50% of your time to business and marketing**. Time that, like your creative habit, has to be spent in a daily practice. Fifty percent of your time should go to reflecting about and doing things that contribute to your work being seen, heard and purchased. Fifty percent of your time should go to planning your business, sketching production schedules, networking, setting up marketing funnels, thinking about your target audience and how to reach them—and putting those strategies into practice.

It might seem a lot now. If you feel the resistance, come back to mindset. Remember what we've established in the last chapter. Business is creative. It is a part of your creative endeavor, as important as is your creative work, no, even an indispensable part of your creative work. It completes your creative practice, because it makes you think about whom you serve, how you can reach them, what products and services you can create for those people that are your ideal audience. And it makes you thrive creatively as you see your efforts reach other people, see them matter to others, and change lives. It will inspire and motivate you to create more, and better.

You feel this initial resistance, I can sense it from my desktop right here as I write these words. Move past it. If you want to establish a creative business for the long-term, you need to think about business and marketing, and you need to dedicate an equal amount of your time to these tasks. Take my word for it. It's worth it. And it will make you a better content creator and storyteller.

But how to establish this daily habit? And what to do during this time to use it effectively? This is the topic of this chapter. I will walk you through the daily business practice that contains these 3 steps:

1. Draw a line
2. Plan and monitor
3. Evaluate and re-adjust

You can use all the strategies of habit building for the daily business practice. The good thing is you don't have to consider the specifications inherent to the creative habit we discussed in the previous chapters. You can just use the good old habit building strategies—the habit loop. Set up an intention implementation. Write down the time and the place when you intend to do your daily business related work, and stick to it.

The danger is that the analytical work, especially in the beginning, is something that meets a lot of resistance with the artist. Your instinct will be to avoid it until you savor the sweet taste of the results. But until the results come, overcome the inner resistance and still do the work. Don't think about it. Just establish a time and place, and do the tasks. Immerse yourself into the strategies. When the first results come flying in, you'll fall in love with it.

It will remain a complicated relationship, just like your own creativity. But just sit down and write a business plan first. Figure out how you want to increase your revenue, how you want your production schedule to look like, what your business funnels are and all the other things that we will talk about in the next chapter. You will see that when you sit down, knowing your strategy and knowing what you aim for, it will be so much fun to analyze and to plan and to implement those strategies in your business.

Step #1: Draw a line

Although content creation and business are two parts that complete each other, in your daily practice you need to separate them. Those two have different goals and different means. Creativity is about creation, about solving creative problems and creating unique content. You don't want to mess with that by at the same time trying to determine how to sell it. This will diminish your creativity and take away from the uniqueness. Reasoning about how to sell it while you create might turn it into something generic and prevent you from taking risks. Risks that are often necessary to create something outstanding.

Just look at Hollywood. Nowadays, most Hollywood productions are remakes and parts two, three, four, five, six of the same franchise. I'm tired of watching superhero movies, be it Marvel or DC. I'm craving something unique. That's why I went to the cinemas twice when Christopher Nolan's new movie came out (I'm also an absolute fangirl, as you might have noticed). But to produce something different takes courage because those things don't come with a guarantee. Remakes and sequels of something that was successful once contain less risk. With new things, you don't know if they will land or not. This is why you don't want a blend between business and creativity too early in the process, or else you might turn into a generic coward.

Instead, wear different hats for each. By doing so, being on the one hand the creative artist and on the other the ambitious businessman or -woman, the efforts will meet somewhere in the middle where the ideal product is forged. How can you separate those two? Draw a line.

Draw a line with time. Many experts advise to do creative work in the mornings and analytical work in the afternoon. In the morning, our subconscious is more active and open for creative work, while in the afternoon, it's easier to think along the lines of analysis, planning and monitoring. So what can you do? If you have a day job, establish a creative habit in the morning before you set off to work and your business practice in the evenings after work, for example. If you have more time to spare, even better. Draw a line by separating the creative and business practice in two different time blocks.

Draw a line with place. You can have two different desks for each or two different desktops. I've heard some creatives operate with two users, one for the writing side and one for their business side, which helps them separate those tasks digitally. Some creatives go as far as having two separate rooms, one for the creative work and another for analytical work. Some go out for their creative work, sit down in cafes or in nature while they perform analytical work at their regular desk. The separation with place can work in smaller or larger ways, whatever is possible for you.

Draw a line in your mind. Wear your business hat when you're considering your business—creatively, of course—but not as the one who creates those things, not as the artist, but as the CEO of the company. Look at the numbers, consider the strategies and come up with creative ways of how to increase those numbers, how to reach more people. Consider, on the other hand, your inner artist as the employee of this business. As a partner who helps the CEO reach these numbers but has his creative side and is the expert in craft. Separate those two in your mind very neatly. When you sit down to perform the creative habit, the CEO hat is off. And when you perform the analytical habit, you move away from the inner artistic child.

Step #2: Plan and monitor

Realistic planning and monitoring is the key to a successful business.

Once you've overcome the resistance and sat down at this appointed place, get clear about your business plan, your goals for the year, the quarter or the week. Be specific in your planning and monitoring.

This part is hard for many creatives. With numbers, we tend to be easygoing. We are content with writing whatever, and if we don't meet this estimated number, we're not particularly bumped. We just want to do the creative work and get better at it. This is why we're here in the first place, right?

Many people hate to work out, but they want to feel healthier and look better. But once they do it regularly, overcome the initial resistance and the mindset of "I hate exercise", find their process, see the results—they come to love it. The same goes for business. Once you overcome the mindset of "I hate marketing/business" and come to terms with seeing yourself as a creative entrepreneur, and once you see the results, you'll be hooked.

With business, be realistic about what you want to achieve, when you want to achieve it, and by what means. Some rough numbers, deliberately thrown together by what you roughly estimate, won't do the trick here. You might dread the hard facts, but only they will make sure you have the right answers for underlying questions like: When will I be able to make a living from my art? How much do I need to make this living? What do I need to do in order to manage that?

If you successfully avoid these hard facts and numbers, and keep going for the next two or three years, you will be disappointed. Because you assumed somehow in the back of your mind that by that time, you would be able to live from your creative endeavors. Trust me on this, I've been there. Success didn't settle in the way I had subconsciously hoped. Why not? Because I didn't write down specific, realistic numbers, and I didn't monitor my efforts to meet them and tweak them to get there.

Don't be afraid of the hard facts. They will set you free. They will show you what you actually need to do to get to your goals, and what timeframe is realistic for it. They will set up the right expectations so you're not thrown if things don't work out like you dreamed they would. Here are some specific questions you must answer with specific numbers:

1. How much money do you need to pay the bills?

First, determine how much life costs for you. How much money you need to pay your bills and expenses and where does the money come from? If you're aiming to quit your day job, you need to analyze what numbers you need to do so. Find out how much it costs for you to make a decent living. If you've quit your day job already, determine where this money will come from. Do you have a side track of commissioned work that will pay your bills? In the beginning, your creative endeavors and products won't be enough. Maybe you have to downsize? Move cities? Adapt a simple lifestyle for the time being?

If you set the goal to pay expenses and bills with your backlist in, let's say three years, you need to establish an estimate of how many products you need to create and how much you need to price them for this to work. And for that, you need to know the minimum amount for you to make an acceptable living.

2. How much do you need to re-invest into your business?

Most of the money you earn from your creative products, you will need to reinvest into your business at the very beginning. Everything has a cost. Website hosting. An email list. Advertising, packaging and other services. Courses that will help you with the learning curve in the beginning—all of those cost money. Expect to reinvest most of the money into your creative business in the beginning. This is the right thing to do, but for that, you need a safety net. Another way to pay the bills (what we talked about in question 1). More than that, this safety net will even fund your business as you start out.

Give yourself a budget for that. How much are you able and willing to reinvest into your business? Where will this money come from and where will it go?

3. How much money do I want to earn?

Pay yourself first. This is what Orna Ross, founder-director of the Alliance of Independent Authors, always teaches in her seminars. Once your backlist generates enough money, you must figure out how much you can and want to pay yourself. Consider it your target salary.

The amount for that plus the amount what you need to reinvest into your company makes up the total sum of what you need to earn per year. The rest will be profit.

4. How do you want to market your products or services, and how much does this cost?

Put aside a budget for marketing. Technically, it's in the reinvestment budget addressed in question two, but I still want to highlight it because marketing is a two-sided coin. You have to spend money on marketing (unless it's content marketing, but those effects are hard to measure), but you also want to make money from marketing. Good marketing has a good ROI (return on investment). Otherwise, it's useless.

So with marketing, you will need to monitor carefully how much you spend and what the return on investment is to make it worthwhile instead of flushing money down the drain—which can easily happen.

You will always need to monitor your money. Where does it come from? Where does it go? If you pay taxes, you will need to get into these details by the end of the year, anyway. Why not analyze them and turn them to your advantage? Use them for planning so you have realistic expectations and production schedules?

You also need to monitor your marketing efforts to see what works, what doesn't and how to tweak it. Marketing is about experimenting and trying things. Not all things that work for one person will work for another, and not all things that work for one product will work for another. So with marketing, be at the top of your game, especially regarding a pay-to-play environment—monitor your marketing to see what works, what to double down on and what to tweak.

Step #3: Evaluate and readjust

Approximately every quarter, you need to reevaluate your business efforts. See if you've met your deadlines and your income goals. If not, why? Maybe you need to tweak them. Maybe your expectations were not realistic. Maybe you need to change your daily routine. You need to evaluate your marketing efforts. What did work and what did not work? Readjust them accordingly.

At least four times a year, readjust your trajectory concerning your business and marketing efforts in order to meet your yearly goals. And when the year ends, you reevaluate your year, think about the goals and accordingly, set them for your business again (more on that in the Yearly Production Planning section).

These are your daily steps for business. Start with planning and then monitor how these plans work out. Evaluate your efforts and then readjust and make a new plan. This is the drill. This is your daily business and marketing practice in general. Of course, you will need to go into the specifics of your particular market and your particular product. But before you can dive into it, you need a business plan. You need a vision.

I found that most business plan templates out there are boring, and when I tried to use them, I never finished. You need a business plan that suits your character and your temper—a business plan for creatives. I divided this plan into three consecutive steps. Turn the page to write an insanely creative business plan that will become a roadmap for your creativity and success.

Your Creative Business Plan

> "Creativity isn't learning the right answers but asking the strongest questions."
>
> Robert McKee, Dialogue

Nine-year-old Rylee's mother found a hand-written note titled "Rylee's Dog Walking Buisness" where the girl wrote a step-by-step business plan to make the endeavor work. With seven steps ranging from *ask parents for help, get them to say yes, print papers with info,* all the way to "Sucsess!!!!!!!" it quickly became an Internet sensation. Even a nine-year-old knows that a successful business needs laid out steps that start with an idea, learning, pricing, marketing and dedicated work. All of this was intuitively in her "buisness plan".

So I hope you have your pen and paper ready as we're nearing the most exciting part of this book: your Creative Business Plan. As you read, I recommend you take notes and write down your thoughts and ideas, stop for a moment and just jot down everything that comes to mind. This is an interactive chapter where we will examine the three ingredients to a creative business plan:

1. Your business vision and overview *(including the mission statement, the big picture goals, the eco-system and story brand)*
2. Your marketing strategy
3. Your yearly production plan

If you want to go deeper, see examples and more visual work on that, get my video course for the Business-Minded Creative at *storymasterclass.com/business-minded-creative-course.*

Disclaimer: I'm not a financial advisor. Far from that. I have my own financial struggles and difficulties, my own issues with money and mindset, but I've learned to deal with them openly and confront my insecurities to fight them. And this is what you should do, too. Confront your mindset concerning money and business. Get to the point where your fingers tickle with excitement as you sit down to write your business plan or your yearly goals and production schedules. Conquering money mindset is a first and huge step to a successful creative career, and it starts right here. With writing down your very own Creative Business Plan.

You must do the work here. I can only guide you this far. Paper and pen ready? No? Then step away for a moment, take a deep breath, make some coffee (the good one, remember?), and re-read the chapter about mindset.

Done? Then let's do this!

1. Your Business Vision and Overview

Start with the big picture before you break it down. The first step to your business plan is seeing it from the bird's-eye view, as if zooming away. Observe your business and creativity as a whole. This perspective is always helpful to return to when you get lost in the labyrinth of details and deadlines. That's why you should always have it at hand—to remind yourself what's at stake here.

Your Business Goals—the Mission Statement

> "Our mission is to empower every person and every organization on the planet to achieve more."

What company does this mission statement belong to? Could be anybody's, really, which gives a clue to the purpose of a mission statement. Let's look at a couple of more for inspiration. By the way, the one above is Microsoft's.

> Squarespace empowers people with creative ideas to succeed.–*Squarespace (obviously)*
>
> To help bring creative projects to life.—*Kickstarter*
>
> Spread ideas.—*TED*
>
> Our mission is to unlock the potential of human creativity — by giving a million creative artists the opportunity to live off their art and billions of fans the opportunity to enjoy and be inspired by it.–*Spotify*

These mission statements alone prove yet again—business is about service to people. It's about building something meaningful, creative, that serves a target audience. Excited about writing your own mission statement yet?

Let's look at a definition. Susan Ward from Balance Small Business writes: "A mission statement articulates a company's purpose. It announces to the world at large why your company exists."

The mission statement is your why, at a very abstract scale. Why do you do the things you do? What are your values behind it? What's the purpose? Remember: this business plan is for your own purposes only. No-one else has to see it. The purpose of this plan is to give you clarity and direction about how to proceed. So speak from the heart here and don't be afraid to dig deeper.

Why do you want to do this in the first place? What difference do you want to make? What drives you? Write it down. Try different versions until you hit the core. Until you know: *that's it.* Let this statement, this purpose, empower you to be better, create more and reach more people.

The Big Picture Business Goals

While we're still in flight mode, zoomed away, let's consider your big picture business goals. Where would you like your business to be in ten or twenty years' time?

Your goals will change over time as you develop and grow as a content creator. Still, it's helpful to peek ahead and determine what your business is all about. Do you want to build a big company with several employees or do you want to stay a solopreneur and instead work with a team of freelancers? How many pieces of content and products do you want to publish in 10 years' time?

I love the saying Joanna Penn has on her wall: "Create a body of work that I'm proud of". I've not peaked into Joanna's house, mind you. Just heard her say it in the podcast. But think about the statement. What you're doing with the business is creating a body of work. What is the body of work you would be proud of? What would you like to create that fills you with joy, pride, and satisfaction? It might be a big company with employees and something that grows far beyond your control. You might also be happy, like I am, with being a solopreneur and having your own desk and your own control over the things you can overlook.

What are the milestones you want to accomplish? Do you want to quit your day job? If so, when? Do you want to provide for your entire family? Do you want your spouse to be able to quit their day job and maybe join you in your endeavors? Perhaps you want to invest and if so, where and how? Do you want to give generously to a cause you believe in?

Don't be afraid to write down money goals. How much money do you want to earn? What kind of business do you want to run in 10 years—six figures, maybe more? Do you want to reach financial independence with your business? Don't avoid giving room to ambition. Ambition drives you.

What are the accomplishments you want to have? How many books do you want to write, for example? How big do you want your YouTube channel to be? Or how many courses do you want to create? How large should your email list be? Don't forget, these are all estimates, rough numbers and therefore only dedicated for you to get clarity about what you want to accomplish and the way you want to go. For now, it's not important how you will achieve these goals. This is what we will talk about in the next steps. It's important to clarify for yourself **what your goals are**. Write them down.

Because if you don't know where you want to go, you might end up somewhere else entirely. Whereas when you have a goal and a map, you will, after a certain amount of time, maybe a detour or two, get there inevitably.

Your Eco-System

Never, ever put all eggs in one basket.

You don't have to be everywhere, especially with social media, but you have to separate your income streams so that your business doesn't break down when one platform does. Your business is an ecosystem. This ecosystem describes all the places where people can find you, your products and whatever you do.

For me, it's my website, all the different retailers you can buy my books on, my podcast, my YouTube channel, my social accounts on Instagram and Facebook (although they only exist, I don't actively do much on social media) and my email list.

Once you have established these platforms, draw a connection between them. Transform them into an interconnected system, ideally in a mind map.

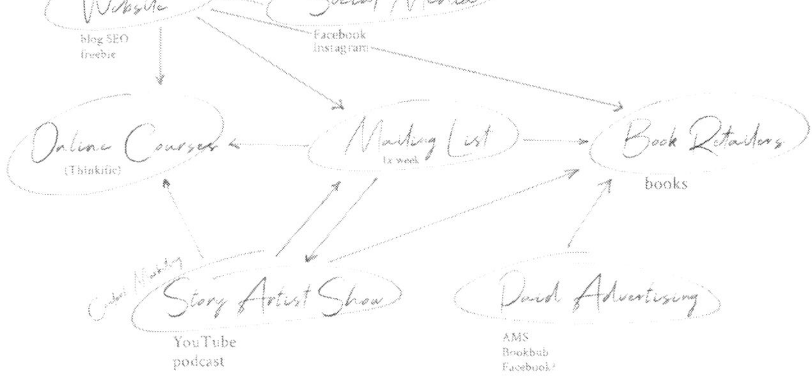

For example, the goal for my website is to get people on my email list and to present my products. My presence on retailers is there to sell my products. My podcast is a content marketing instrument. Of course, there's more to my podcast—knowledge for me, value I and my listeners derive from it—but its primary purpose is content marketing, and again, to get people to sign up to my mailing list. The same goes for my social accounts and YouTube. I want to gather followers, no question, but as long as those followers remain on the platform, they're out of my control. This is why I always want to direct them to, you've guessed it, my mailing list. It is my primary marketing instrument (more on that later.) And from this mailing list, I refer to the vendors selling my products, my courses, and my books, ask to follow me on social and so on. This is how the ecosystem is interconnected.

Think about your own ecosystem. On what platforms do you want to be found? Again, you don't need to be everywhere. I highly discourage it. Ask yourself: does it make sense for me to be on this platform? Do I want to be doing YouTube? Do I need my own website? And what's the point of my website? Do I want it to be something that is searchable on Google and competing in SEO? Or is it just a landing page where I direct people to sign up to my mailing list? Do I really want to be doing a podcast? Write down all of your possibilities and then think carefully about what makes sense for your business. Don't do everything just because everybody else does it. I tried, and I failed.

Instead, think in terms of minimalism here. I always advocate for a minimalistic platform building strategy, and if you've read the "Storyteller's Blueprint", you'll know. Ideally, pick three places where you want to be found, those that make sense the most, and stick to them. Don't try to be everywhere. Focus on three platforms instead and do them really well.

Your story brand

This is my favorite part because we will be talking about storytelling. And because, when I grasped the concept of story branding, it revolutionized the way I approached my business. There's an entire book written on that topic, "Building a Story Brand" by Donald Miller. But as a passionate storyteller, let me try to explain the concept to you.

The story brand is all about the story you're telling your audience. And the most important thing to understand is that your customer, your reader, your audience—they are the hero of the story. It's not you. As much as you'd like to be the hero—and let's be honest, we're always the heroes of our own musings—it's time to turn the tide here. Your brand story revolves around your ideal customer and around their path from A to B.

What's a story? A story is a journey from A to B, has a beginning, a middle and an end. It's an adventure of a main character. And it's always about change.

> "Stories are the creative conversion of life itself into a more powerful, clearer, more meaningful experience. They are the currency of human contact."
>
> Robert McKee

The situation cannot remain the same. As cannot your hero. By the end of the story, profound change has to occur. This is the same with story branding and story marketing.

Your hero, your customer, he or she is now caught up in their Ordinary World. What is this Ordinary World? What is their situation? You have to establish that at the very beginning. What problems do they face? What anxieties do they harbor? And the most important question: what's their desire? What is driving them? If you understand their desire, you'll be way ahead of many others. And as you know from storytelling, desire is the most important part of a story. What does the hero want? What does your audience want?

This is where the villain comes in. The villain is somebody or something that prevents them from having what they want. For example, my audience are content creators who want to be heard, to share their creativity with the world. This is their desire—to connect, to find their tribe. The primary villain is the noise all around us. The internet where people are shouting into their megaphones, wanting to be heard. This noise drowns out the creations and the stories of the hero—my audience—preventing her from reaching her goal. The noise is their greatest enemy. Define the greatest enemy, the villain who's attacking your audience's weakness. Who or what is preventing them from getting what they want? And once you have established that, you have defined the main conflict of your story. A content creator who wants to be heard, but is drowned by the noise. This is the conflict in my story brand. What is yours?

But please, don't stop here. Go for the inner conflict as well, because in a good story, there are always two types of conflict: the outer and the inner conflict. The inner conflict is hidden deeper inside the hero himself, a fear, a deep seated anxiety, doubts or wrong mindsets. To get where they want to get—to conquer the villain—they need also to resolve the inner conflict that is holding them back. For example, with content creators, it's imposter syndrome. It's the fear that they're not good enough and that their story does not deserve a platform. And this you need to know and address as well in your story brand.

Here's where you come in. What's your role in this story? You are the mentor. You're somebody who's there to guide them out of their problem towards a solution.

This framework works with everything. Even when we talk about sheer entertainment and fiction. Your audience are genre lovers drowning in this dull world and looking for escape and entertainment, or maybe looking to make sense of this world in a certain way. You as a fiction writer are their mentor. You want to provide them with entertainment and escape from the problems of this world, you have the solution.

If you analyze my landing page on storyartist.me, you will notice that it's build upon these exact storytelling principles. I establish the conflict, both outer and inner. And then I offer the solution. My solution is, drumroll, ... storytelling. Because storytelling is embedded in human DNA. It is the best possibility to be heard in a noisy world. And the same goes for you and your story brand—in the story you're telling, you are the mentor who swoops in with the solution being your products and your services.

Story is about emotions, not facts.

Why do you think people are happy to pay hundreds of dollars for a sneaker that initially in production costs dozens? Because they're telling themselves a story, a story they believed because of this particular branding. They're telling themselves the story that they're able to run better and look cooler. The prices are not justified by how much effort and production cost were originally put inside. The story builds the value instead (plus also an expected amount of quality—you don't want the sneakers to fall apart after a week of wearing them, after all).

So what story do you want to tell your audience? It's connected to your mission statement. Reflect on it and write it down. Define the elements of your story branding: your hero (the target audience and their desire), your villain (the main obstacle), your conflicts. And define the solution and resolution of those conflicts.

As you position yourself, present the story to the world so it spreads like a wildfire. Because stories are something we cannot escape from. They're inside of us. And if we, as business owners, can tell a good story and make our customer believe it, we have won her over. To make her believe, it has to be well-crafted and authentic throughout. In every detail and every minor element. Live and believe it yourself. Embed it into your brand design, even your personality. If you're able to, they will be delighted to be part of the story and they will readily accept their role as the hero.

These are the things that define your overall business.

- the mission statement
- the big picture business goals
- the ecosystem
- the story brand

Once you've worked them out, you are ready to dive deeper into marketing—you strategy to reach your audience. How you want to position yourself in this noisy world so that the right people—your heroes—find themselves in the middle of your story.

2. Your Marketing Strategy

Let's talk about marketing. The ugly, unpopular word nobody wants to utter in the artistic gathering. But you know better now, right?

Marketing shouldn't spark disgust and diversion inside of you, and set off your escape mechanisms. Your inner alarm shouldn't wail while the word tickles your ears. Instead, it should excite you. It means that you get to offer value to the people that want it, that you get to find your tribe, your people, connect and spread the word about the story you want to tell. This mind shift is essential. I urge you to keep fighting the wrong mindset about marketing until you adapt a childlike sense of excitement when you hear this word. It will empower you as a content creator, setting you apart from most creatives out there.

In classical terms, the marketing funnel has four stages: awareness, interest, desire and action. In the beginning, people have no clue who you are. So you first need their *awareness,* need them to at least notice you, then show *interest* in what you do, and spark a *desire* in them that gets them to take *action*—which is buying a product, subscribing to your email list, and so on. I'd like to add a fifth stage of the marketing funnel that I discovered in Pat Flynn's *Superfans.*

> "Focusing on the experiences that create superfans is more important than any other activity in your business."
>
> Pat Flynn, Superfans

Finding your superfans should be your target. You don't want people to only take action once—as in buying your product or subscribing to your email list. Although there will be people who only do that. But this is not enough to build a sustainable business. You want people to connect with you on a personal level, people who are so enchanted by what you do and who you are they buy every single one of your products. This is the connection that you desire. Not everybody, by far, will become a superfan. And that's okay. Because as most already know from Kevin Kelly, you only need one thousand of them. Once you reach your one thousand true fans, your business will thrive.

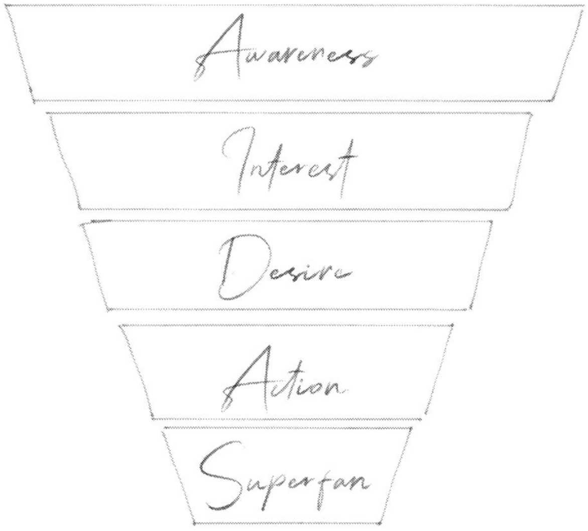

Most creators focus their marketing efforts largely on awareness. But this is only the first step in a long funnel. Instead, focus your efforts on the whole funnel, from awareness to action, and finally, to a growing number of superfans. How you want to design those funnel stages is up to you. How do you want people to become aware of you? How do you want to attract their attention?

There are different forms of marketing for that. For example, **paid advertising** on several platforms—Facebook, Amazon and others where your fans are to be found. Paid advertising as a quick way to raise awareness, but it also costs money and time because it requires a lot of testing, especially in the beginning. Not all forms of paid advertising work for everybody. Still, most entrepreneurs nowadays argue that you need to adapt the pay-to-play environment to get noticed in this overcrowded world, because platforms increasingly push paid advertisement.

Then, there's **content marketing**. Content marketing means that you're providing valuable and great content and thus sparking people's awareness about who you are, awakening their interest to know more about you. The good thing about content marketing is that it's free. The downside: it takes time to pick up momentum and to bring results. My favorite form of content marketing is SEO—writing blog posts that are searchable on Google. I'm convinced that SEO can be a very powerful tool when done right. And also, of course, there's YouTube, podcasting, social media, which also is a part of content marketing until you build a certain number of followers and can include advertising or sponsorship to turn it into revenue streams.

Another one is **networking and collaborations**. You can, for example, appear on different podcasts, which is great fun and doesn't involve a lot of investment on your part. Collaborative projects and marketing efforts with creatives in your niche, and connection in general, provide a value on both sides. And this can be a powerful form of marketing, especially if you tap into another creative's audience that is larger than yours. For example, if I listen to podcast episodes with guests I like, I'm very likely to buy their books or products. But networking needs to be genuine. You don't want to be yet another spammer. Genuine networking takes time. Don't go out and email a bunch of people asking them for links, likes and shares. Instead, start following people, start connecting with them on a genuine level, asking questions, trying to be helpful. And then, when the time is right, asking for a favor.

While paid advertising is about awareness, content marketing and networking covers also interest, and may even get as far as desire because it includes value—free content or knowledge that you give away in the form of blog posts, interviews, giveaways, YouTube videos, social media content and everything else. And in this context, content should spark desire to take a certain action.

In my opinion, this action should primarily get people on your **email list**. Your email list is one of the greatest marketing tools that you own and have control over.

> "Any author that has tried any kind of promotion will tell you that nothing converts like email. Even if we consider the biggest promo tools available to any authors today, if you look at something like BookBub, the reason why a BookBub featured deal will convert way better than any other form of advertising or promotion is because it's delivered by email. There's something inherent in email which is intimate and personal and it just converts way better. The conversion rate on something like a featured deal is crazy. It's around 50%. Once someone clicks on that deal in the BookBub email, around 50% of that traffic that will arrive on Amazon will actually purchase the book. And you will not get numbers like that anywhere, not even close. There's something about email that just really converts. [...] So the real value of your platform lies in your email list because no other audience, be it on the blog or on any social media channel, will convert in the way your email list audience will convert. No other audience has such a personal connection to you and is able to build such a personal relationship than the audience in your email list."
>
> David Gaughran on the Story Artist Podcast

At the back of every book, at the end of every blog post or podcast episode, I direct the people to my mailing list. This list is my marketing tool for interest, desire and action with upcoming products. I provide the people on the list with exceptional emails, weekly or semi-weekly. They contain value and entertainment, are wired for connection and generous giving. And if I give more than I take, and then ask for a favor, offer a product, ask for a review, they're more likely to grant me that favor.

Look at the marketing funnel. Think about how you can get people from awareness to superfans. It's a lengthy process, but it all comes down to being generous, being authentic, connecting with people on a personal level, answering emails, giving them way more than you ask for and always going the extra mile. Surprise your people with creative acts of generousness and helpfulness. Give them an escape, give them something regular that they come back to and that they can get entertainment and value from. If you offer that regularly, and if you make an effort to go the extra mile, you will get people from the beginning of the funnel to the very end, and find your superfans—your tribe.

Now, it's your turn:

- *What marketing instruments do you want to use for what stages of the funnel?*
- *Where is your target audience to be found – social media platforms, other experts in your niche, Google Search Engine?*
- *What marketing efforts will covert in the long run—for your business—and get people from awareness to superfans?*

Remember: marketing starts with experimenting. Test strategies. Be creative about your efforts and don't give up if things don't work out. Marketing is about finding creative solutions that will reach your tribe. And also, about telling an outstanding, skilled story – because storytelling is embedded in our DNA and we just can't ignore a great story.

3. Your Yearly Production Plan

Now that you know what your overall brand is, how you want to market it and how you want to reach the heroes of your story, it's time for an action plan. Your business, after all, is content *creation*.

What are the products or services that you're offering? In order to make money from your creativity, you need to offer something that people will pay for. This is not only a necessity. It's good for your customers, too. Don't believe me?

Have you ever got something for free and never opened it again? I know I have, and so did you. Why? Because it was free. Because it had no value to you. You didn't pay for it. It was thrown at you when you thought you were interested, but you never made the time to work through it or dive deeper. Especially if it's something extensive, like a course, something that requires a lot of time and effort.

If people haven't paid for it, they're likely to never work through it. On the other hand, when people pay a decent amount of money for something, they value it. They look at it in a different light.

Have you ever found a deal, online or in a store, and thought: *This too good to be true, it has to have a catch*? You don't really trust that deal because it just seems too cheap for what they're offering. But if something is expensive, it increases in value in your eyes. You assume,

Okay, if it's that expensive, it has to be good, right? The same goes for online products. With pricing, never undervalue your work. People will lose their trust. They'll assume it's too good to be true. And the value of your work in their eyes will decrease.

Whereas when they assume that it's reasonably priced, maybe even a little expensive, they'll believe there's value behind it. Of course, you must deliver. Even over-deliver, if possible. Because if people pay and don't get what you promised, they'll be disappointed—you will lose potential fans and your reputation.

So what's a good rule of thumb when it comes so pricing? Ask for a little more than you're comfortable with. Think about it like that: people pay for a solution to an urgent problem. They will gladly pay a price that they can afford in order to get what they desire. This is why —side note—when you're offering the solution, you never advertise with what people need, but with what they want. You don't advertise a product that will help get a daily workout habit in six weeks; you advertise a sixpack in six weeks.

What are the products and services you will be offering to your audience? What meets their most urgent wants? Those products make up your backlist. The largest part of your body of work. And this is created year after year.

That's why you need a yearly production schedule. But I found that a year is just too big to oversee. Too many things can happen over the course of 12 months, things you never planned for and couldn't have anticipated. Deadlines you didn't hit and have to move up. So instead, **have a vision for a year and a plan for 12 weeks.**

In "The 12 Week Year", Brian P. Moran recommends reframing your annual mindset, and instead defining your year as 12 weeks because it's a manageable time-span. Twelve weeks fit neatly into your mind, divide your year in four quarters, and provide an opportunity to work towards goals set for those four quarters.

> "We mistakenly believe that there is a lot of time left in the year, and we act accordingly. We lack a sense of urgency, not realizing that every week is important, every day is important, every moment is important. Ultimately, effective execution happens daily and weekly!"
>
> Brian P. Moran, The 12 Week Year

Come up with a 12-week production schedule that is realistic for your situation and temperament. Take your own deadlines seriously because you take yourself and your professional work seriously. If you have a vision for this year to, let's say, write four books or create some pieces of content regularly, email weekly aso., consider the timeframes like you would in a day job. You would work extra hours to get to a deadline and be responsible to your boss and client. Do the same with your creative business.

If the goals you set yourself and the production schedule just wear you out, go back to it, and with a new, realistic mindset, adjust it so it fits into your lifestyle. And then again, take your deadlines seriously. After a while, you will learn what you can do in a week, in a month, or in 12 weeks. For example, I'm always over ambitious and I need to slow myself down and be realistic about what I can achieve. But on the other hand, I also need to motivate myself and provide some positive stress in terms of deadlines, so I finish my work and don't postpone it indefinitely.

Consider how much you want to earn from these products and give yourself a financial goal for those 12 weeks. Consider investments, ongoing costs, and your own salary. Like I mentioned before, don't forget to pay yourself separately. Solopreneurs have a difficult time separating themselves from their business. Start with accounts—at least two different ones for your business and your private expenses. Pay yourself a salary. In the beginning, you will very likely need to reinvest everything that you earn from your business. As discussed in this chapter, you will need it to make money and pay your bills from a side track—the services that you provide additionally, or the freelance work you do on the side. But set yourself this goal—to increase the salary that comes from your creative business, bit by bit.

So here's what your yearly plan needs:

1. A vision for the year

These are the products and services that you want to offer and create in this particular year, then the deadlines and the production schedule where you distribute those products and services onto a timeframe so you have an overview of what you need to accomplish every quarter of the year.

Be realistic when you consider your daily creative and business practice. How much time can you dedicate daily to both? If you only have 15-30 Minutes daily, your goal could simply be to write a book and sell it. This is fine, too. It's just impossible to write four books with such a small amount of time.

Your vision can also include skills you want to learn, travels and vacations you want to make, and maybe even a mindset you want to address.

2. A project-based plan for 12 weeks

Your daily practice, the one you learned to establish early on in this book, is what will ultimately drive your production schedule for the 12 weeks. Dedicate each week or even a couple of weeks to **one single project.**

I am a scattered creative who is interested in so many things and would love to write books, create courses and direct plays simultaneously. But this approach lacks focus. And it steals productivity and effectiveness. Now, I work on one single project during my creative practice until it's finished, and then move on to the next. Additionally, I try to align my business practice to support that project. For example, if I'm writing a book during the creative time, I work on the package and promotional strategies for that book during the business time—setting up the launch, booking giveaways, commissioning the cover design and so on.

The launch of the product is always the deadline, and from there, I move to the next creative endeavor. Bit by bit, day by day, I build my body of work. This is the power of a yearly plan that stems from a clear vision, both for your overall business and your year, and a project-based 12 week schedule.

Let's recap. These are the three steps to writing your creative business plan:

1. Your Overall Business Plan
2. Your Marketing Strategy
3. Your Yearly Production Plan

Most importantly, don't forget to be creative.

Dream big. Don't be afraid to ask the questions concerning your values, your dreams and desires for the future. Don't be afraid to get excited about all the possibilities that open up before you. If you plan them right, they can become reality. And this is the difference between only dreams and tangible achievable goals.

Start out dreaming. But continue planning.

Never forget your big picture, your core values that will accompany your business into the next decades. Get creative about the marketing possibilities. Analyze the market, look at what others do. They don't always tell you how and why they do it, but if you are able to open your eyes and look at what's visible in plain sight, you will discover the strategies that work. Don't be afraid to take another road and try something creative, something entirely different from what everybody is doing, like Somerset Maugham did. There are best practices, but there are also risks, and successful people can combine both.

Do unusual things. Things other people never think of, or are too afraid to put into action. Get creative about your marketing strategies.

The same with a yearly plan. It's a blueprint for you, not something rigid, but something living and breathing as is the business plan itself. It's only a step to get you closer to your big picture goals, but it's a huge step. Think about what you can do in a year—you can finish a book series, you can publish and sell courses, you can grow your YouTube audience by thousands.

And while you incorporate these things, consider the story you want to tell and the heroes of your story. Never make the mistake of thinking about your audience as just another number. Behind every number is a person with concerns, emotions, passions and ideas. Picture instead a thousand heroes, each of them with their own unique story, giving you the privilege to live out your creativity and shape theirs. And this is a privilege never to be taken lightly. You get to share your story, but you also get to shape the story of others.

You see, a business plan is something creative, personal, and absolutely exciting. It's an adventure. If you consider this adventure a road trip, then the business plan is your map that points to the sites you want to visit, the paths you want to take. Every one of them as exciting as the next. And there is no actual destination, this is the beauty of it. The journey of being a content creator is a journey of becoming, every step as beautiful as the next, every stop on your adventure as exciting and enriching as the next.

A road trip is not just about rushing through your stops to get to the airport and back home. It's about enjoying every step of the way. It's about taking in every milestone, every site. And this is how you should view your creative journey and your business plan. It's a road trip with amazing stops and an adventure where you're not entirely sure where it will take you, but at the same time, you know that it brings you closer to your dreams.

PART IV

The three pillars of a future-proof creative

Years ago, we build a massive church building for our community. The foyer on the first floor is lined with thick, white pillars. They are positioned strategically to hold the massive service hall above, constructed for over eight hundred people. As this is a charismatic church, the services are loud, and people dance and jump to the rhythm of the worship music. If you happen to be standing on the ground floor while hundreds of people jump above, you might notice the ground shaking. Wobbling up and down to the rhythm of the music. And fear for your life. Yet the construction will never break down, because the exactly right amount of pillars shaped in the exactly right way were positioned on the exactly right places. There are few of them, therefore it's easy to assume that the entire building might crash. But they are enough.

Over the years, I've found that if you build your creative career on three pillars, your business will hold, even when it's tested to its limits. And it will be tested. Unexpected things will hit you. Pandemics, economic crashes, personal tragedies. Technology will evolve. The market will change, maybe faster than you think. But as long as the pillars stand, so will you.

These pillars are **perseverance, practice and purpose**. You need all three of them to grow a meaningful business that will withstand the test of time, crisis, and creative wastelands. None of them can stand on their own. Perseverance without a clear purpose and daily practice? Nope. Practice without purpose and perseverance… you get the picture. Let's look at each of them in detail so you understand what I mean.

Perseverance

A friend of mine recently gave birth to her very first child. I could tell that she was struggling, but the way she framed her everyday battle stuck with me. "Life's not like in the Pampers adverts," she said.

Inside, we have hidden expectations about how our lives should look like. Expectations formed subconsciously by our upbringing, culture, and media. We expect our wedding to look like Instagram, our apartment like Pinterest, and life with a new baby like a Pampers advert. But wrong expectations ruin careers, marriages, relationships, and lives. When I got married, I knew marriage would be hard. But I didn't expect it to be *that* hard. I didn't expect my first child to alter my life *this* massively. I didn't expect my first years as an online entrepreneur to go *this* badly.

You do prepare for difficulty. But somehow the high of the excitement about this new adventure suggests: maybe you'll be spared from the abyss? After all, the lady in the Pampers advert makes it look so easy. The illusion of the ecstatic feeling of standing at the altar, holding your baby, or finishing your first book, is so alluring that you are tempted to think it will never wear off. And when it does, you're disappointed.

Remember the fateful morning when I admitted to my husband

and to myself that I was too tired to go on? The one where I was tempted to give up? On that morning, I asked a question. A question that held a certain finality. One I had to answer—before admitting to my defeat and going back to a day job.

What's the single most important trait that makes successful creatives?

I asked my online mentors for their secret ingredient. The answers were surprisingly unanimous. And unglamorous. There is a secret of success, I discovered. But it's not a magic wand. It's something that challenged me at exactly the point where I needed it most.

> "Diligence. The ability to wake up every morning and do the work is key. You can't control how you feel about what you're doing. You can't always control the results of what you're doing. But you can always control what you're doing and the fact that you are doing it. Putting the emphasis and the enjoyment in the work rather than the immediate results allows you to be patient as you persevere."
>
> K. M. Weiland

> "Persistence. Everything else can be learned."
>
> Joanna Penn

> "Without a doubt, perseverance. You have to be gritty and willing to toil in obscurity, have books that bomb, and make mistakes. That's how every great success story begins. You only lose if you give up."
>
> J. Thorn

They might have used different terms. But they all meant one thing. The only secret of success is perseverance. *You only lose if you give up.* A knot tightened in my throat as I read the answers. Wasn't it what I was about to do? Give up. Get a day job. Live like "everybody else".

A writer I knew put her self-publishing career on hold and explained it in a blog post. She called self-publishing a "fast-food book industry", angry with the writing-fast model and the emerging pay-to-play environment, blaming scammers, readers, and fellow writers. There was bitterness in this post. A bitterness I understood. Self-publishing is far from a dreamy vision of everybody can become a famous author overnight. The online world feels cruel to creatives. I felt her pain that morning. I still feel it now.

Could it really be that simple? Just keep going and you'll succeed one day? I dug deeper. Analyzed the answers Katie, Joanna, and J had generously given me. Looked into what others had to say. How can we persist in the face of the terrible things that might even threaten our existence? Is there a right way to persevere? These are the 4 secrets I discovered. Secrets that will enable you to persevere.

Edison's secret to perseverance: reframing

Thomas Edison was considered unteachable at a young age. When he set out to create the electric light bulb, most thought he failed. But he chose to frame it differently.

In *The Danish Way of Parenting* the authors set out to discover why the Danes are the happiest nation in the world. One technique they pinpoint in the book is "reframing".

Reframing means to change an imagined or emotional viewpoint about how a situation is experienced and viewing it differently.

> "If you ask a Dane about the weather when it is freezing, gray, and raining outside, they will unwittingly answer: 'There is no bad weather, only bad clothing' or 'I am glad we can get cozy inside at home tonight.' If you say, 'Too bad it's the last day of our vacation,' they might reply, 'Yes, but it is the first day of the rest of our lives.' If

> you try to get them to focus on something really negative about any topic, you may be mystified at the way they can reinterpret it."
>
> *-The Danish Way of Parenting.*

Reframing is not about ignoring reality or running from problems by pretending they're not there. In fact, Danes can be brutally realistic about life, as we know from the dark Scandinavian movies. But it's about changing your language when you face a problem and thus changing the way you view this problem. Because language is the frame through which we see the world.

Do you know how Edison framed his so-called failure? He simply said he found over 1,000 ways to not build a light bulb. Have you found 1000 ways to not tell a story? To not market your product? Or are you tempted to give up at the third so-called "failure"? *Every great success story begins with making mistakes.* Maybe the most realistic expectation is that your fall will be greater than you think. That you'll fail harder than you ever thought you could. And that it's okay. Because in truth, it will be your ladder to success. You 999th way to not build a lightbulb. The first day of the rest of your life as a great storyteller.

Paralysis by Analysis

A year ago, we moved apartments. When I entered the new place, I could barely get in because boxes stood *everywhere.* Stacked in every room. Especially in the spacious entrance area, too inviting to carry any box past there. My first reaction was paralysis. Luckily, I learned the solution to that kind of situation from my mom and quickly switched mindsets. But not my husband. The poor guy stood lost amidst all boxes, staring at me. I smiled and told him to get the rest of the things with the guys while I'd handle the situation. *Just start with one thing.* This was my mom's voice inside my head. So I did focus on this one task: getting the right boxes into the right room, and out of the entrance area. When my husband returned 30 minutes later, he was mystified by how different the apartment looked. The chaos was gone, and the setup allowed an overview of what to do next.

A common way that forces us to give up is paralysis by analysis. Paralysis by analysis is the state of over-analyzing (or over-thinking) a situation so that a decision or action is never taken, in effect paralyzing the outcome.

We all felt it. When the task in its entirety seems too overwhelming and you don't even know where to start. This ugly feeling sitting in your gut, a feeling that urges you to take flight instead of confronting it. The enormity of the big picture paralyzes you. Establishing a creative career is a task too enormous to face. You need a catalogue of at least 10 products, a website, a mailing list, networks, social media, online courses, paid advertisement and content marketing. Even the broken down tasks on their own paralyze. Writing a book, for example. The idea, the process, the tagline, the cover, the blurb, the outline, the first draft, editing, language, research... the list is endless. If you consider it in all its enormity—or compare yourself to those who have been in the industry for over a decade—paralysis by analysis hits you. It hits you hard. And it tells you to throw the towel.

John Grisham's secret to perseverance: a single simple intention

John Grisham wrote 45 titles. Which is 1.4 books per year. Do you think it was the focus of his career to write 45 titles? If it was, we would have never heard of him. And this would be a shame because his novels are brilliant.

John Grisham has a secret. It's a simple intention that he focuses on every single day: write at least one page per day. One page per day is 365 pages per year. Which is around 1.5 novels. Which are 45 titles in thirty years. Alright, we did the math, and you probably instantly sense the overwhelm coming back. What do you mean—thirty years? Just focus here with me. Focus on this one page. Every. Single. Day.

Every week, I break down my daily task to one single focus. Record a video. Publish a post. Setup Ads. When I focus my day on one thing, I know I will get it done. If I try to cram more inside, I will fail, and most likely procrastinate because I subconsciously feel the paralysis. A single simple intention is a secret to perseverance. Focus on a daily small result that moves the needle. What will be yours today?

You can't control how you feel

In Film School, we were told that you shall never, ever, direct an actor by using feelings.

"Act as if you were angry."
"You're very sad about this situation."
"This new information makes you happy."

If you ever hear a director talk like this—you know he's a fraud. Why is this such a big faux pas? Because people can't control what they're feeling. Emotions come to us without having asked for permission. They overwhelm us, some caused by things, some just out of the blue. And we cannot decide on them. We cannot make ourselves feel happy.

Remember what author K. M. Weiland said: "Diligence. [...] You can't control how you feel about what you're doing. You can always control what you're doing and the fact that you are doing it." Read it again. *You can't control how you feel about what you're doing.*

To accept the fact that you can't control your feelings about your creative endeavors means going from amateur to professional. The problem is: artists often chase the high. The moment when they feel the kiss of the muse and the itching in their fingers to start the work. This is the mindset of an amateur. Feelings change moment to moment, minute to minute. A professional refuses to be defined by feelings. When on this fateful morning, I stared at the high debt on my bank account, I felt tired. Defeated. But was I? It was a feeling, and now I had a choice to make. Do I act on that feeling? Or do I choose to persevere?

Tony Robbins' secret to perseverance: the ultimate power

Tony Robbins, probably the most successful motivational speaker who started his career as early as 17 years of age, promotes the philosophy of decision.

> "Decision is the ultimate power."
>
> Tony Robbins

He calls decision the "ultimate power" because in the moment of your decisions and the actions you take accordingly, your destiny is shaped. Learn to step away from your feelings when they're not getting you where you want to go. When you feel like an impostor. Like a failure. Like a fraud. When you want to give up. Instead, pull from the power of decision by asking yourself:

- *How do I want my daily life to look like?*
- *How do I want my life to look like in 5, 10, 20 years?*

Then decide accordingly. Choose to create time and time again. Fail. Fail better. This is the secret to perseverance.

Why the process is crucial

It was night in Paris. Robert Daniel sat behind bars in a station house, angry with himself.

This was where his temper got him. This was where his dream of becoming a professional wrestler got him. He was good. The problem was his personality. Got him far in wrestling, but not far in life. He had wrestled down a police officer this night. Just imagine—a police officer! He had felt like a hero. But the feeling didn't last very long. Stupid, that's what it was. He realized it now, in this cold cell where he couldn't even lie down for a few hours of sleep. Maybe it was time to give up.

The morning crept in like a hyena, eating away the dreams that had died that night. Robert gathered his belongings, meandering to the exit and to his apartment. His head ached. He was tired. *Time to give up, buddy.*

But what now? All those years of training—for nothing? What would he even do with his life? Find a decent job, wear a bowtie? He dropped into his bed, never appreciating his old mattress more. He would look ridiculous in a bowtie. The phone rang. He picked up. Maybe they wanted to summon him to court now.

"Robert Daniel?" His name sounded absurd in a French accent.

"Yes."

"Here's the Police Sports Foundation."

Robert held his breath. The sports foundation? The man on the other end continued: "Your qualities as a wrestler have raised some tumult here this morning. We would like to invite you to perform at our charity event next week."

We all heard the hackneyed phrase: "Love the process." The problem is: the process isn't always very lovable, as the true story above shows. It mostly doesn't consist of Eureka moments and charity events. It entails metaphorical prisons and cold, uncomfortable nights. It's filled with failure and doubt, rejection, poverty, and the always present whisper to just give up. And yet, exactly this process is crucial. Why?

According to multiple studies, about 70% of all lottery winners end up going broke and filing for bankruptcy. Those people lack the process. They didn't earn it. They lack the years of hard work, failure, trial and error, and experience necessary to become the people they need to be in order to handle such an amount of money.

The secret of the process is that you need to change in order to deal with your success wisely. To get where you want to get, you need to become another person. A better version of yourself. Yes, there are ways to optimize the process. But when you find yourself in those situations where it feels like you're caught behind bars, like you failed again, and the small voice whispers inside of you, *Time to give up, buddy,* remember that all of this is part of the process to transform you into that person you need to become to be successful. And that success might just be around the corner.

Perseverance is one of the indispensable pillars that will hold your creative business during tough times. Only those who persevere, those who refuse to give up when things get difficult, but pivot and alter their business and their approach to the changing waves of time, again and again, stick around for years and decades successfully. *You only lose if you give up.* Have you found your 1000 ways to not build a lightbulb yet?

Practice

What do you need to run a successful creative business? A new MacBook? A new mic to start a podcast? A new camera to start a YouTube channel?

Famously, every business starts in a garage. A garage that represents the fact that the equipment is unprofessional, that there's no money for the next fancy thing. Remember, Stephen King wrote his breakthrough novel in a laundry room and J. K. Rowling in a cafe next door. George R. R. Martin still writes on a DOS computer, and James Patterson on yellow paper with a black pen. The famous YouTuber Casey Neistat shot on extremely bad cameras, but it didn't prevent him from exploding his channel. What do these creatives have in common?

Practice.

Your level of success is not defined by your equipment. And let the lack of it never be an excuse to forgo practice. Practice is the next important pillar for success. There is no substitute for hard work, not even with a fancy piece of equipment.

We talked a lot in this book about how to establish a creative and business related daily practice. But all of this will remain useless if you don't put the theory into, well, practice. No one else can do it for you. Knowledge is not enough. We all know that it's better to work out instead of sitting on the couch, read instead of watching Netflix, and eat the salad instead of the burger. But only few *practice* it. And without practice, theory is useless. Even the Bible says that "faith by itself, if it does not have works, is dead" (James 2,17). This is no coincidence. People are wired this way. We know things. But we don't act on them. And even if we do, it's mostly an impulse that doesn't last very long. This is why the first pillar is perseverance, by the way.

Practice requires intentionality and often the sheer habit of sitting down and doing the damn thing. No revelation from above. No supernatural kiss of the muse. No angel that appears to you in your sleep. Just the simple knowledge of what is right and putting it into practice. After a while, if you persevere, it will become a habit. But at the beginning, it's pretty damn hard. And you will derail from your habit again and again, and again.

As we already went into depth about how to establish the practice, I just want to remind you: establish a creative daily practice that works around your lifestyle. No matter how busy you are. Even if it's 15 minutes in the morning and in the evening. More, if you can manage it, but start with what's possible for you. Better 5 minutes than nothing. Once you get into the habit, once you get the taste, increasing the number will be much easier.

Newton's first law of motion states that "an object at rest stays at rest and an object in motion stays in motion with the same speed and in the same direction unless acted upon by an unbalanced force." To get started, to get yourself from the state of rest into the state of motion, force is required. You must add energy. This is normal, it's the laws of physics, after all. Once you're in motion, no energy is needed anymore. But you have to keep the momentum. If you lose it—well, you'll need force again. Simple, isn't it? The daily habit ensures that you don't lose momentum. That once you started writing this book, you work on it every day. Once you started the blog, you work on it every day. The momentum keeps you going, helps you stay in motion without extra force needed to keep the practice. But in the beginning, and if you get lost—apply force. Put in energy. Get into motion and let the laws of physics work in your favor.

The Plateau of Latent Potential

In *Atomic Habits,* James Clear introduces the idea of the *Plateau of Latent Potential.* Countless things in life seem to not to make a visible difference until they reach a certain point of breakthrough. Cancer spends 80 percent of its life undetectable until it takes over the body in months. Bamboo can barely been seen for five years before it shoots up ninety feet into the air within six weeks. Similarly, habits appear to make no difference, seem to have no tangible results for a very long time. That's why people give up easily.

> "It is the human equivalent of geological pressure. Two tectonic plates can grind against one another for millions of years, the tension slowly building all the while. Then, one day, they rub each other once again, in the same fashion they have for ages, but this time, the tension is too great. An earthquake erupts. Change can take years–before it happens all at once. Mastery requires patience."
>
> James Clear, Atomic Habits

Remember: The daily practice is what really counts. If you show up every single day to do the work, it will accumulate. And if added perseverance—break through, eventually.

Nora Roberts writes a book in 45 days. She's so prolific, in fact, that under the additional pen name J.D. Robb, she writes a series of romantic, futuristic police stories featuring Detective Eve Dallas. She writes romances because they are easy to write and sell, and puts her own spin on the stories. Roberts earns more than $60 million per year, and her books are almost always on the New York Times bestseller list. She earned that success with hard work and practice. I mean… a book in 45 days. This is incredible. Interestingly, Nora still lives in the house she moved into as a nineteen-year-old bride. So much on fancy stuff.

Purpose

David Seidler was born in London in 1937. As a child he fled the London Blitz, traveling to America with his family on a three-ship convoy. German U-boats sank one of those ships. This traumatic experience made David develop a stammer, something that would plague him for a very long time. No speech-therapy helped. He withdrew, grew quiet, afraid that people would notice his flaw and make fun of it. At the age of sixteen, he decided he was done hiding, and set out to become a writer—since communication through the written word came easier to him. King George VI, who stuttered badly, sparked his particular interest. David began to collect information on the king and Lionel Logue, the king's unconventional speech therapist, determined to also use his own experiences as a stutterer to tell the king's story. In 2005, he started writing the script that became The King's Speech—a movie that won four Oscars, including Best Original Screenplay.

But this was not his purpose. The purpose he had writing this story was mirrored by what people who struggled with the same problem wrote to him: how much it meant to see someone in a movie triumph over stuttering and how grateful they were that a fellow sufferer could give them all a voice.

If you are driven by a purpose higher than yourself, you will find your tribe and be able to persist.

I started learning how to play the piano when I was seven years old. I loved it when it worked smoothly, but I was also a kid who would get frustrated easily, ready to throw the towel any minute. It went so far that I developed the impression that my entire body itched when I failed to play a piece. But my mom would not budge. She stood next to the piano, and forced me to return to that chair, and play again. It would have been easy for her to just let me quit. Who wants to deal with a hysterical child that claims her whole body itches? But my mom had a purpose. She didn't want me to be a star pianist, mind you. She wanted me to develop character. To push through and persevere, even when things got difficult. And I will always be grateful for that.

Always know the purpose behind your creative business and never lose sight of it. Especially when things get difficult. Many people think that the question of why is overestimated. I'm not one of them. I am convinced that knowing why you want to do this, the deep purpose behind the creative endeavor, will get you through tough times, both financially and creatively. We all hit a low. We all experience difficulties. But understanding and following the purpose will make sure that the creative business represents who you are. And thus will be the only way to proceed.

Why do you want to build a creative business? Why do you want to have an artistic career? The reasons can be manifold: freedom, fulfillment. But I encourage you to look beyond. Look what makes you come alive AND has something to offer to the world, just like David Seidler did. Always remember why. And bring it into your identity. Because only if this represents who you really are will you see your creative business come alive.

I am a thriving artist.

How hard is this to say out loud? Practice. Until you believe it. Until it's part of your identity. Write this out where you can see it until it becomes who you are.

A thriving artist.
A creative business owner.

How to prepare for the future

Es Devlin is a designer known for creating large-scale performative sculptures and environments that fuse music, language and light in collaboration with artists like Beyoncé, Adele and U2. One of her projects was "Poem Portraits". She used 25 million words of nineteenth-century poetry to train a machine-learning model, then combined it with words donated by a gallery audience of 1500 people. She called the result "a collaboration between the living and the dead". Author Yudhanjaya Wijeratne used openly artificial intelligence to co-write his sci-fi novel, *The Salvage Crew.*

No matter what you think about projects like these—collaborations between AI and creatives, the use of new technology that comes up with mind blowing results, tools still unimaginable to us—the future is coming. And it's coming fast.

OpenAI's text generating AI GPT-3 wrote a short film—even with a twist at the end. GPT-3 has gotten a lot of buzz since its release in June 2020. It's been used to post comments on Reddit, write a poem roasting Elon Musk, and even an entire article in *The Guardian*. When the system learned to autocomplete images without having been specifically trained to do so, it even got people speculating whether

GPT-3 might be the gateway to artificial general intelligence. And it wrote a screenplay.

Without wanting to spoiler too much, because you should see it (trust me, you should)—it's a little weird, as one would expect from AI, but it's also very entertaining. In film school, I saw stuff like this all the time. The three-and-half-minute short film called "Solicitors" shows a man knocking on a woman's door and sharing a story about an accident he was in. The prevailing question is: would you have known that an AI generated the story? And if you knew, would you care?

Changes are approaching that will disrupt the creative industry. The pandemic, being one of them, has also accelerated the development of futuristic tools and algorithms. I'm not writing this to scare you. Instead, I include this section to open a new perspective on what will be possible in the future for creative entrepreneurs if they ride the wave of change.

How haunting is the possibility of a collaboration between the living and the dead? How exciting to shoot a short film that was written for you in seconds? Tools are coming our way we cannot comprehend yet, and they will revolutionize the industry. But timeless and perennial principles will remain. And if you base your creative business upon them while trying to ride the wave of change, use the tools to your advantage instead of frantically trying to stick to old patterns, so will you.

My parents don't even really understand what I do for a living. Is this even a career? Most people on this planet don't even believe that money can be made the way we do. With art. With digital online platforms. Yet time and time again, creative entrepreneurs prove them wrong. Those who pioneer change. Those who don't give up.

And this is what I love about this career. It's not just a career. It's a lifestyle. It's a mission. It's at the heart of our life's work, deeply connected with the people we serve and the world we seek to change. We get to control how we react to the surrounding changes. The gatekeepers are largely gone, or about to be removed from most creative industries. We decide how we make our art work, how we continue to serve our tribe.

At the end of the interview with Joanna, we spoke about how to ride this incredible wave of change that's inevitably coming to get all of us.

> "The best way to prepare is to double down on being human and put yourself out there so that it's clear who you are, what you do, what you care about, and so that people can choose you. [...] If we think about the future, we have to say: okay, here's me. Here's my face. Here's my smile. Here are my books. Here's my stuff. And connect."
>
> Joanna Penn on the Story Artist Podcast

Double down on being human and connect. This is what the future will be all about—personal, powerful, and authentic stories.

And now it's your turn. Go out there and tell your story. Every day. Authentically. Professionally. Be bold, be human, and impact the world with your creative business. It needs you more than you know.

Need a guide to find and tell your story?

Note: Please don't forget to leave an honest review on your favorite platform.

I know you have an amazing story to tell, whether you are a writer, video content creator, entrepreneur, designer, musician. You want to make an impact. Build a tribe. Find an audience and make a change. Because this is what a true storyteller does. He changes things to become better.

Start with my free ebook and mini-course, the Storyteller's Blueprint at: **storyartist.me**

Here's what's inside:

- *why an idea is not enough and what you need instead*
- *the 4 most important storytelling principles*
- *the only question you need to answer to live your creative dream life*
- *7 techniques that will catapult your storytelling to the next level*
- *the secret weapon of storytelling*
- *the 3 steps of minimalistic platform building*
- *how to double down on results in less time*
- *how to make money from your creativity*

About Diana Wink

Diana Wink, also writing as D. F. Wink, is an author of dark dystopian fiction and inspirational non-fiction for storytellers and content creators.

She is a podcaster, blogger, YouTuber, film and theatre director and passionate storyteller. In her spare time, she explores theaters, cities and wilderness with her bearded dancer husband and her pumpkin baby girl.

Her website storyartist.me helps people create content that will stand out and connect to a dedicated audience through the power of storytelling.

Want to dive deeper into the topic? Check out the video course on „Th Business Minded Creative" at **storymasterclass.com**

Appendix 1: Bibliography

Find all the books I refer to below.

Atomic Habits: An Easy & Proven Way to Build Good Habits & Break Bad Ones – James Clear

Bored and Brilliant: How Spacing Out Can Unlock Your Most Productive & Creative Self – Manoush Zomorodi

Building a StoryBrand: Clarify Your Message So Customers Will Listen – Donald Miller

Deep Work: Rules for Focused Success in a Distracted World – Cal Newport

Dialogue: The Art of Verbal Action for Page, Stage, and Screen – Robert McKee

Indistractable: How to Control Your Attention and Choose Your Life – Nir Eyal

On Writing: A Memoir of the Craft – Stephen King

Quarter Life Calling: Pursuing Your God-Given Purpose In Your Twenties – Paul Sohn

So Good They Can't Ignore You: Why Skills Trump Passion in the Quest for Work You Love – Cal Newport

The 12 Week Year: Get More Done in 12 Weeks than Others Do in 12 Months – Brian P. Moran

The Artist's Way: A Spiritual Path to Higher Creativity – Julia Cameron

The Creative Habit: Learn It and Use It for Life – Twyla Tharp

The Danish Way of Parenting: What the Happiest People in the World Know About Raising Confident, Capable Kids – Jessica Joelle Alexander

Strangers To Superfans: A Marketing Guide to The Reader Journey – David Gaughran

The Power of Habit: Why We Do What We Do in Life and Business – Charles Duhigg

Superfans: The Easy Way to Stand Out, Grow Your Tribe, and Build a Successful Business – Pat Flynn

Appendix 2: Resources by Chapter

1.2 The gift of perspective

Find the Story Artist Podcast here, on YouTube or on your favorite Podcast App: https://storyartist.me/podcast/

This is Joanna Penn's course *Business Plan for Authors*: https://creative-penn-courses.teachable.com/?affcode=18062_k5zwmbwm

2.1 The Sweet Spot

Alex Newton's Amazon reports: https://k-lytics.com

The Creative Penn Podcast episode on *Beautiful Ebook Formatting:* https://www.thecreativepenn.com/2017/01/09/beautiful-ebook-formatting/

Vellum – the book formatting software for Mac: https://vellum.pub

Find my YouTube channel here: https://cutt.ly/youtubestory

Quarter Life Calling: Pursuing Your God-Given Purpose In Your Twenties – Paul Sohn

2.2 Learning Islands

The World Economic Forum report on The Future of Jobs and Skills: https://reports.weforum.org/future-of-jobs-2016/chapter-1-the-future-of-jobs-and-skills/

The Creative Penn Podcast episode on *Mental Models For Writers And The Empowered Indie Author:* https://www.thecreativepenn.com/2020/10/12/empowered-indie-author/

Bored and Brilliant: How Spacing Out Can Unlock Your Most Productive & Creative Self – Manoush Zomorodi

2.3.1 The Creative Habit

Atomic Habits: An Easy & Proven Way to Build Good Habits & Break Bad Ones – James Clear

The Power of Habit: Why We Do What We Do in Life and Business – Charles Duhigg

2.3.2. Triggers for Creatives

On Writing: A Memoir of the Craft – Stephen King

Routines of famous writers:
https://jamesclear.com/daily-routines-writers
https://medium.com/the-mission/the-daily-routine-of-20-famous-writers-and-how-you-can-use-them-to-succeed-1603f52fbb77

The Creative Habit: Learn It and Use It for Life – Twyla Tharp

About healthy lighting: https://www.archdaily.com/917345/what-is-healthy-lighting

2.3.3. The Battle Plan

Deep Work: Rules for Focused Success in a Distracted World – Cal Newport

Study "The Cost of Interrupted Work: More Speed and Stress": https://www.ics.uci.edu/~gmark/chi08-mark.pdf

Indistractable: How to Control Your Attention and Choose Your Life – Nir Eyal

2.3.4 Seven hacks to get out of a rut

The Artist's Way: A Spiritual Path to Higher Creativity – Julia Cameron

3.1 Lies you believed

Eva Stories Instagram channel: https://www.instagram.com/eva.stories/

An in-depth article about Eva Stories: https://www.campaignlive.co.uk/article/saatchi-saatchi-new-creators-showcase-next-generation-storytellers/1590908

3.4. Your Creative Business Plan

Dialogue: The Art of Verbal Action for Page, Stage, and Screen – Robert McKee

Rylee's Dog Walking Business: https://www.dailyedge.ie/business-plan-2344116-Sep2015/

3.4.1 Your Business Vision and Overview

Article "How to write a mission statement with examples": https://www.thebalancesmb.com/how-to-write-a-mission-statement-2948001

My free ebook and course "Storyteller's Blueprint": https://storyartist.me/free/

Building a StoryBrand: Clarify Your Message So Customers Will Listen – Donald Miller

3.4.2 Your Marketing Strategy

Superfans: The Easy Way to Stand Out, Grow Your Tribe, and Build a Successful Business – Pat Flynn

Strangers To Superfans: A Marketing Guide to The Reader Journey – David Gaughran

3.4.3 Your Yearly Production Schedule

The 12 Week Year: Get More Done in 12 Weeks than Others Do in 12 Months – Brian P. Moran

4.1 Perseverance

The Danish Way of Parenting: What the Happiest People in the World Know About Raising Confident, Capable Kids – Jessica Joelle Alexander

How Failure Taught Edison to Repeatedly Innovate: https://www.forbes.com/sites/nathanfurr/2011/06/09/how-failure-taught-edison-to-repeatedly-innovate/

John Grisham's Do's and Don'ts for Writing Popular Fiction: https://www.nytimes.com/2017/05/31/books/review/john-grishams-tips-how-to-write-fiction.html

Focus: Your First Decision, article by Tony Robbins: https://www.tonyrobbins.com/first-decision-focus/

4.3 Purpose

David Seidler, 'The King's Speech' writer, and his commoner cause: https://www.latimes.com/archives/la-xpm-2010-dec-09-la-en-seidler-20101209-story.html

Final Words: How to prepare for the future

Poem Portraits by Es Devlin: https://artsexperiments.withgoogle.com/poemportraits

"Solicitors", the short film written by AI: https://www.youtube.com/watch?v=AmX3GDJ47wo

Acknowledgments

A special thank you goes out to Joanna Penn – my online mentor who, for the most part unknowingly, shaped my career with her content and her personality.

I am also thankful to my readers, those who have accompanied me on this journey, tolerating my mistakes and failures and stuck around through tough times.

As always, I'm thankful to my Lord and Savior who encouraged, led me through difficulties and inspired me to go on bold adventures and roads taken by few.

Printed in Great Britain
by Amazon

73955268R00097